I see Daleside as a lost town. With few jobs and few opportunities, the future seems hopeless. Roads and houses are falling into decay. The rich families already left years ago—sold their homes and went looking for better places to live. The families that stay in Daleside are mostly the ones who can't afford to go anywhere else. They can't escape from this place. I believe the people of Daleside dream of a better, different life. But, their reality wakes them up all the time. They are static dreamers, stuck in this town, in their lives and in their social class.

They seem to be stuck in their dreams.

For me, there is something universal and timeless about Daleside. It's hard to determine the date and location of when and where the photographs were taken. This is what fascinates me about this body of work. Daleside embodies the decadence of a world.

The more I immersed myself the more I saw the patterns are the same as those I have observed elsewhere. Daleside could be a town in Texas, a small village in northern France, a city in Ukraine or a farm town in Australia.

The population in Daleside, like in so many other communities in the world, suffers from a lack of education and opportunity. Alcohol and drugs fill the void for some people. Religion fills it for many others. Violence and abuse cause more violence and abuse. Often, these cycles of abuse last for generations. The lack of resources and work puts the society of Daleside under an inevitable collective tension. The lack of investment in education deepens the existing inequality. Lindokuhle used to say that the underprivileged people in Daleside had the same issues as the impoverished people in Thokoza, his township. I think that's true. The reality is different, but the issues are the same. That made me realise that social inequalities are what deeply divides a society. Social justice is what we really have to fight for, here and everywhere.

STATIC DREAMS

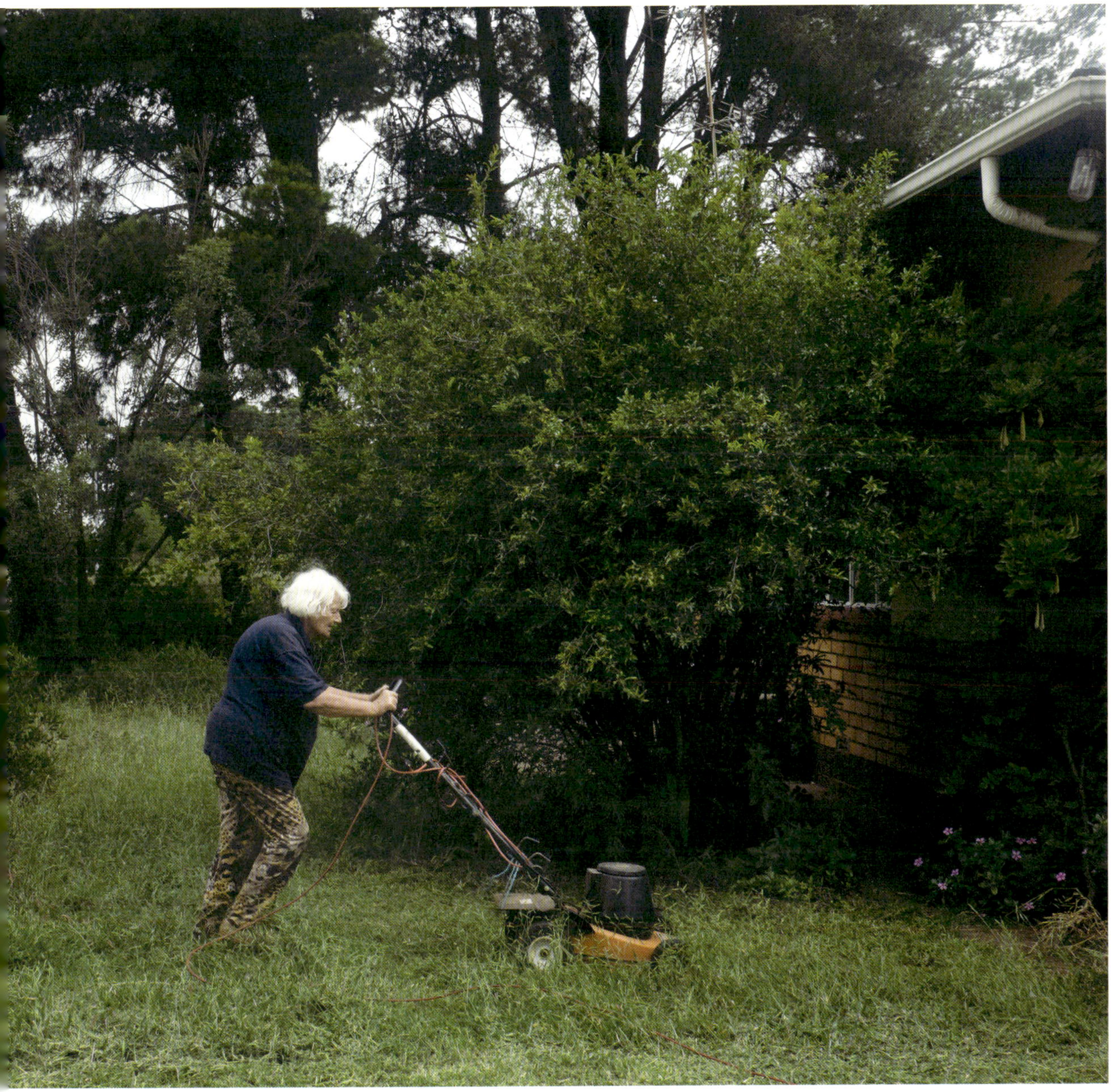

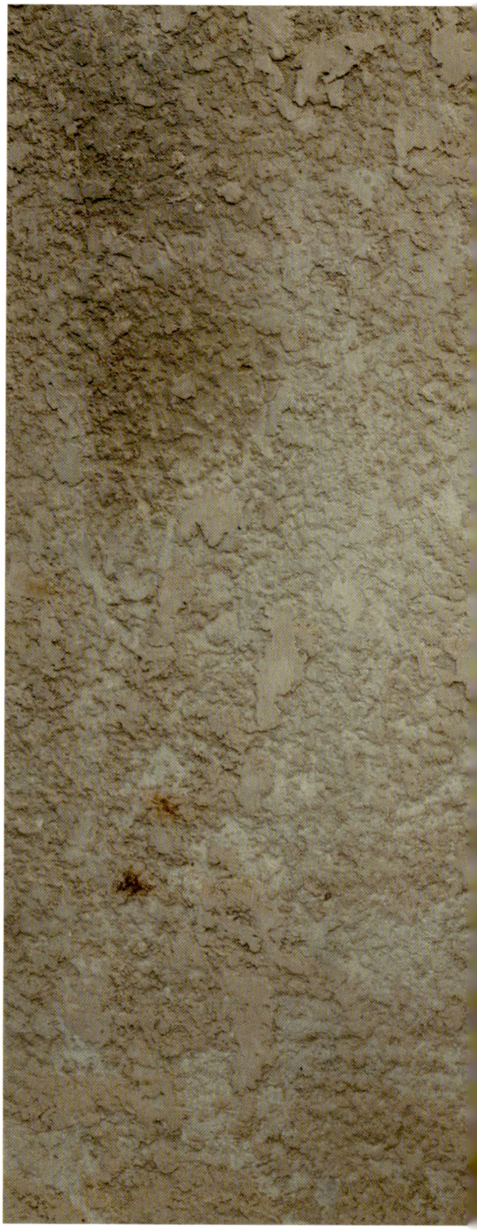

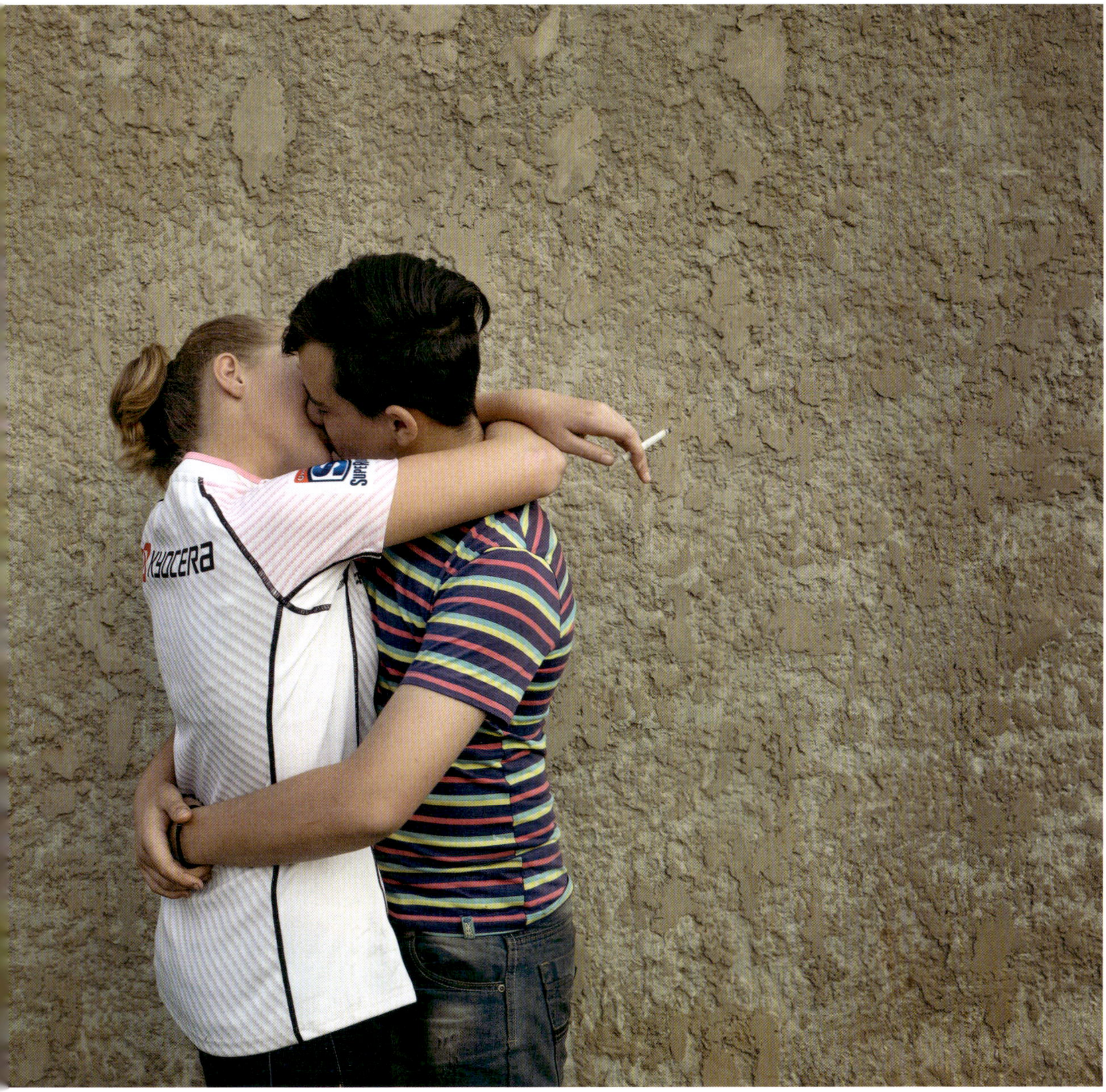
KYOCERA

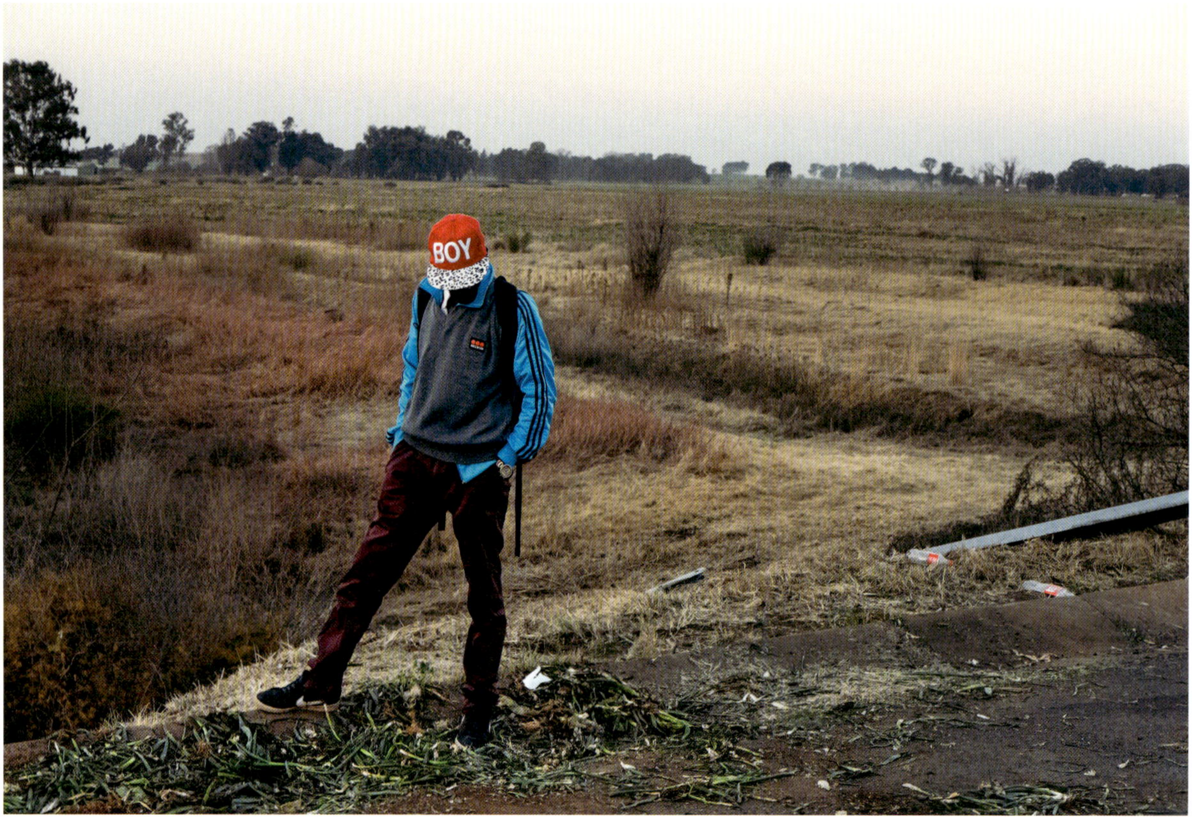
BOY

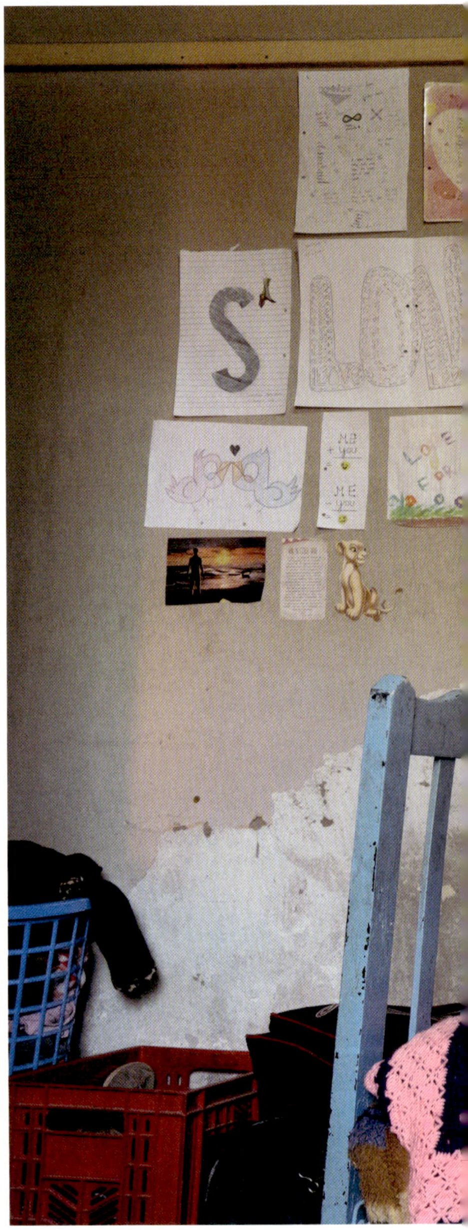

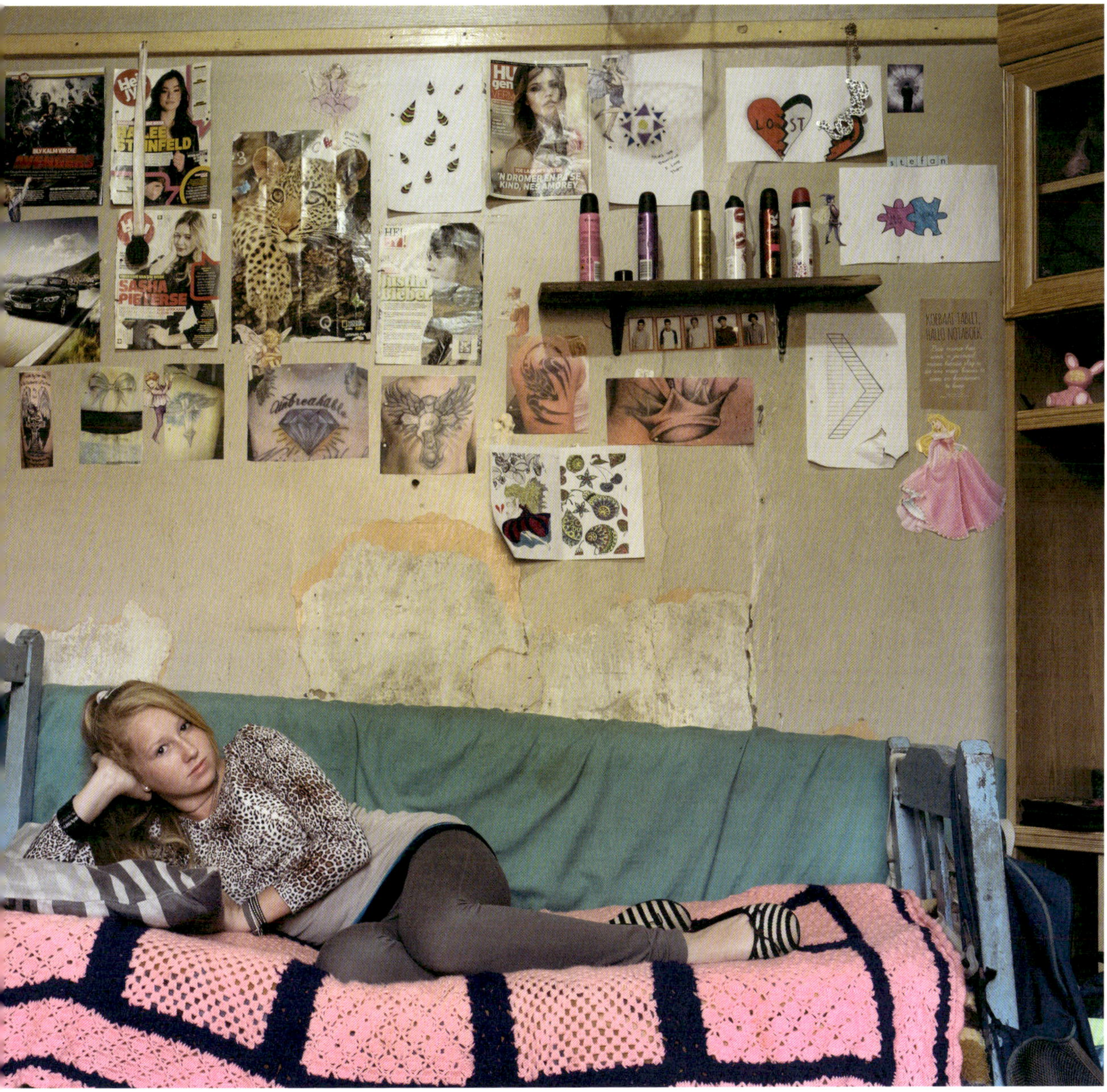

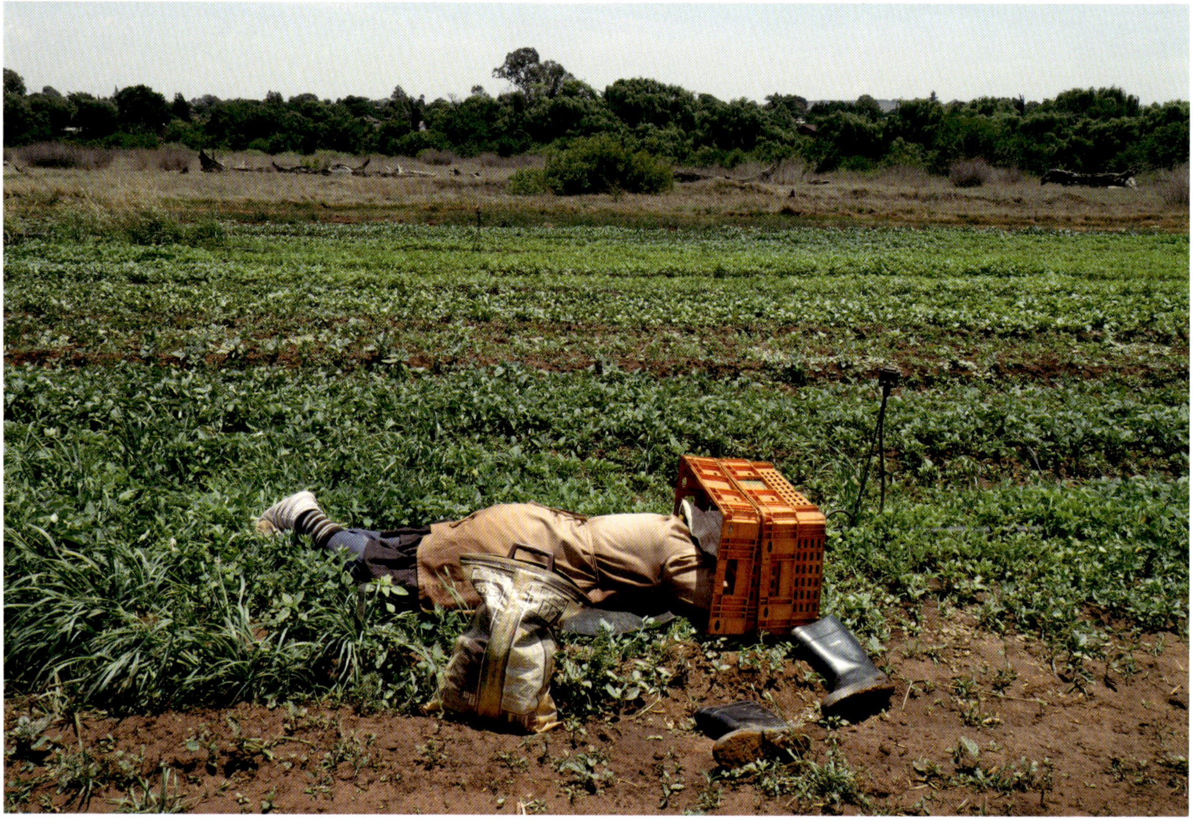

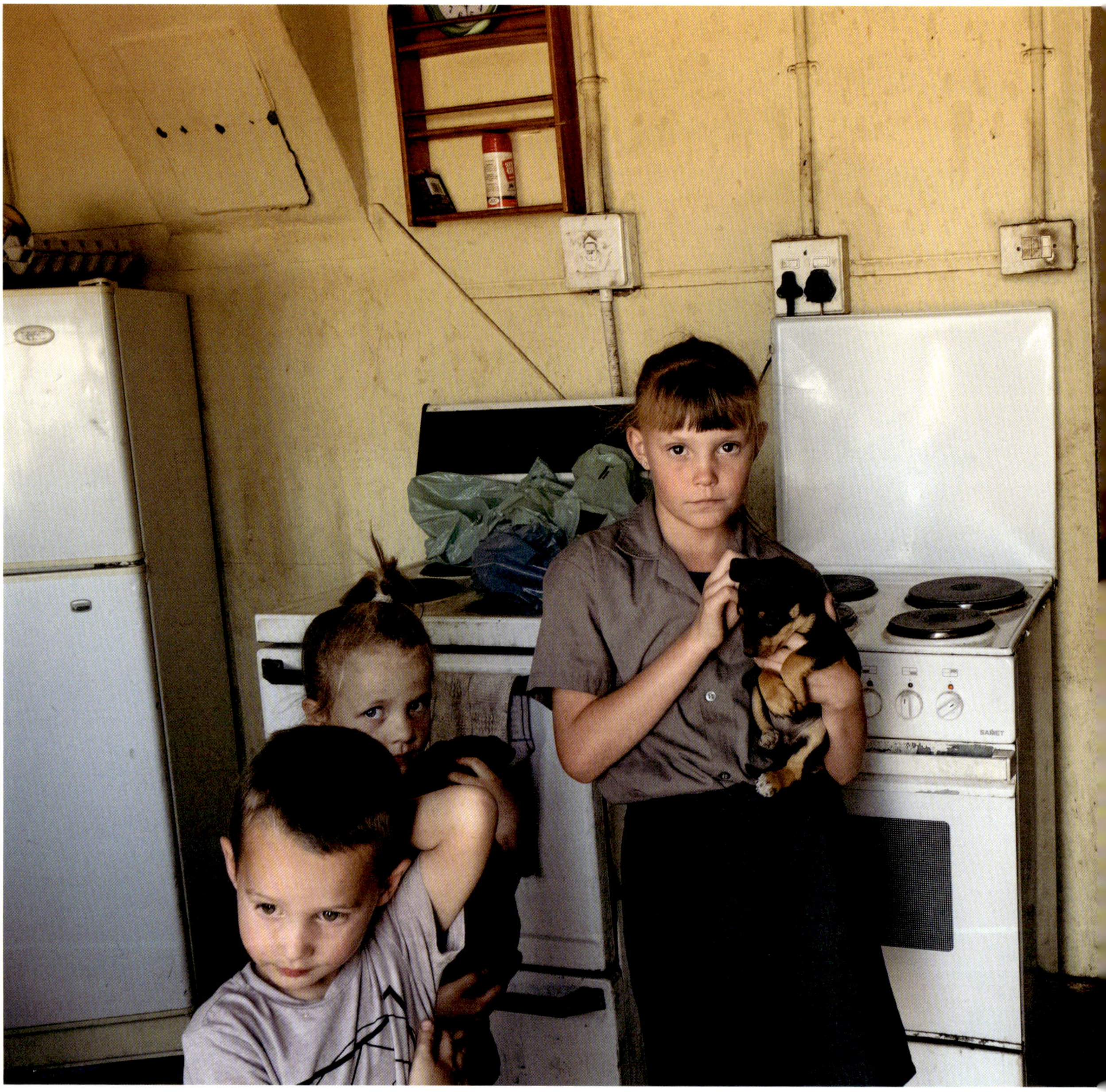

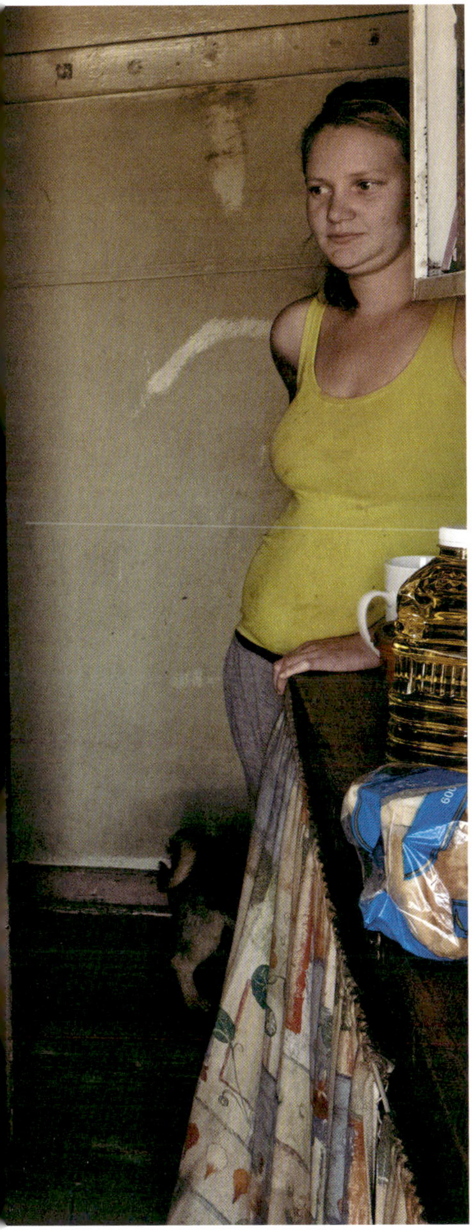

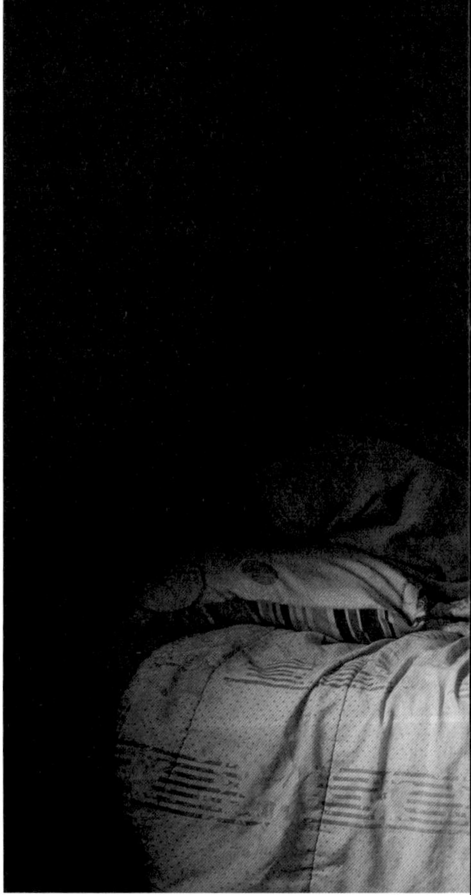

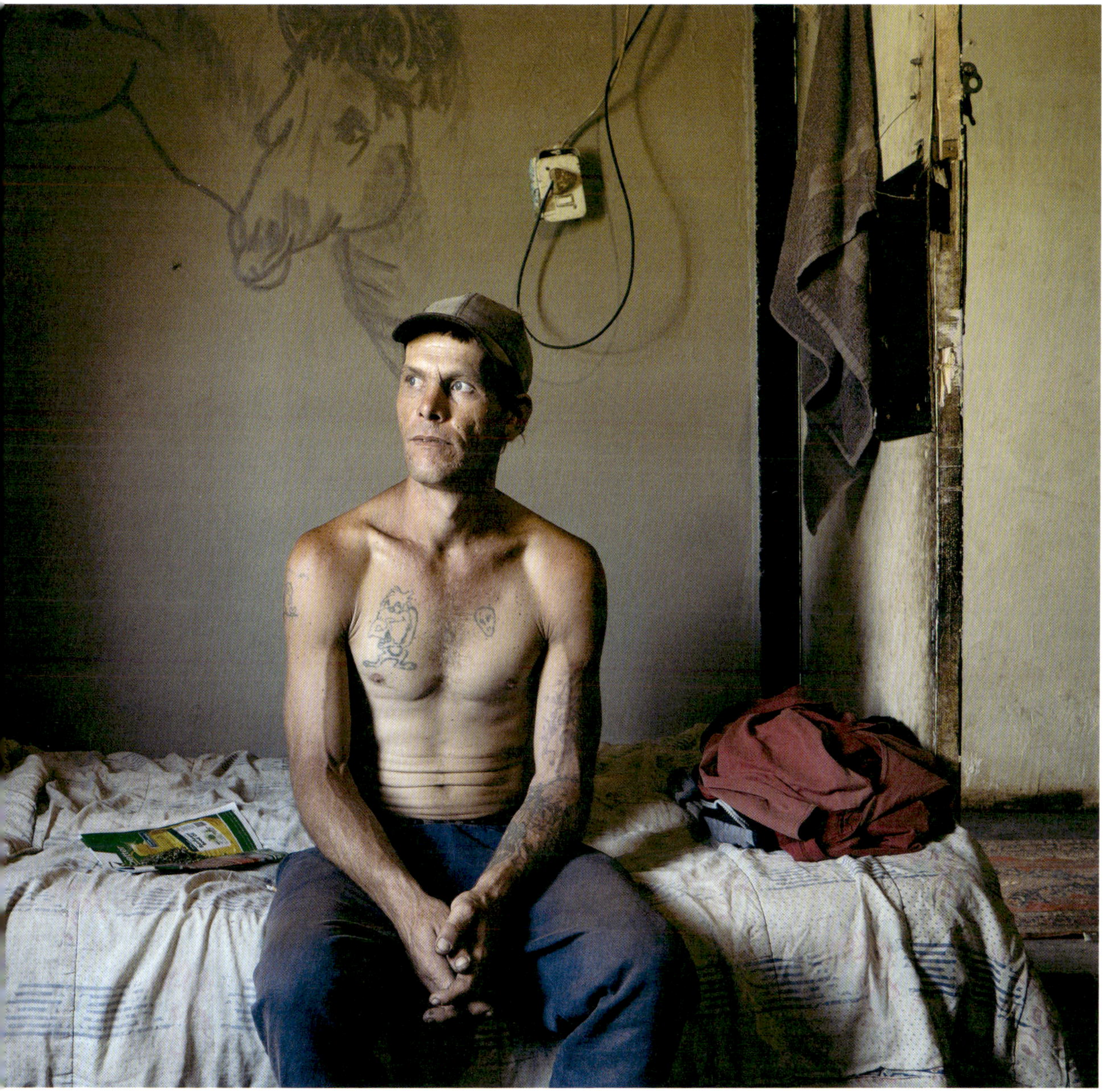

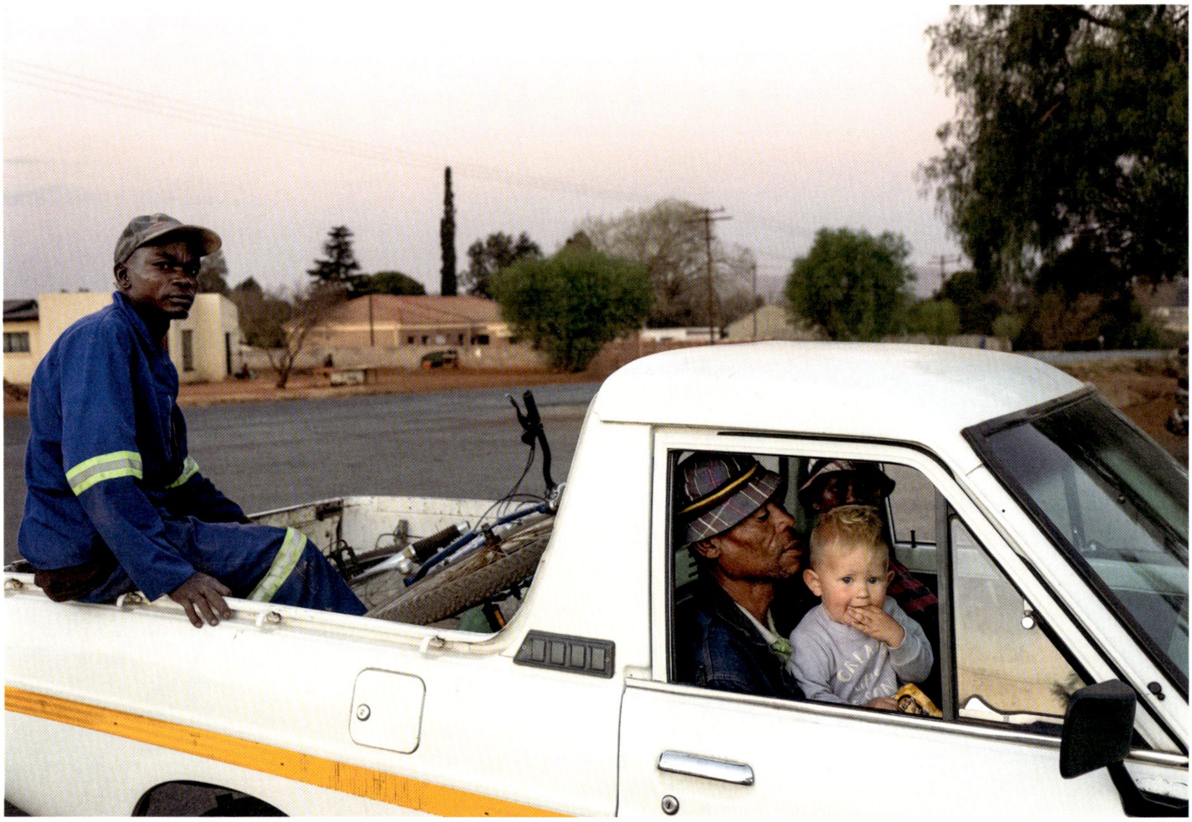

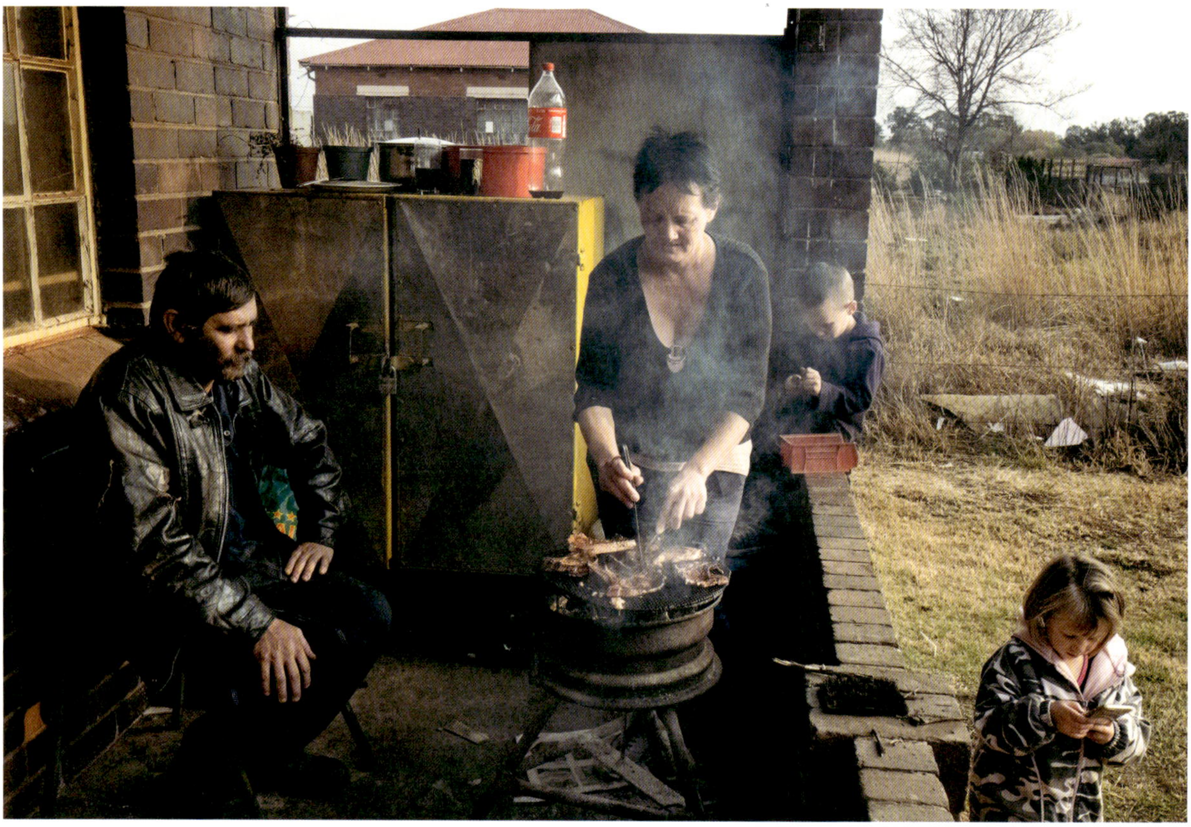

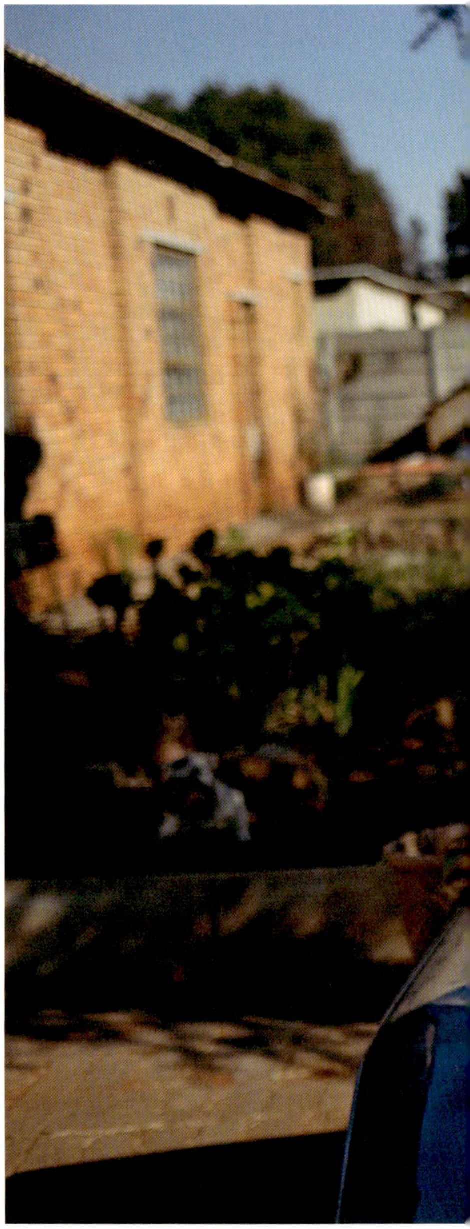

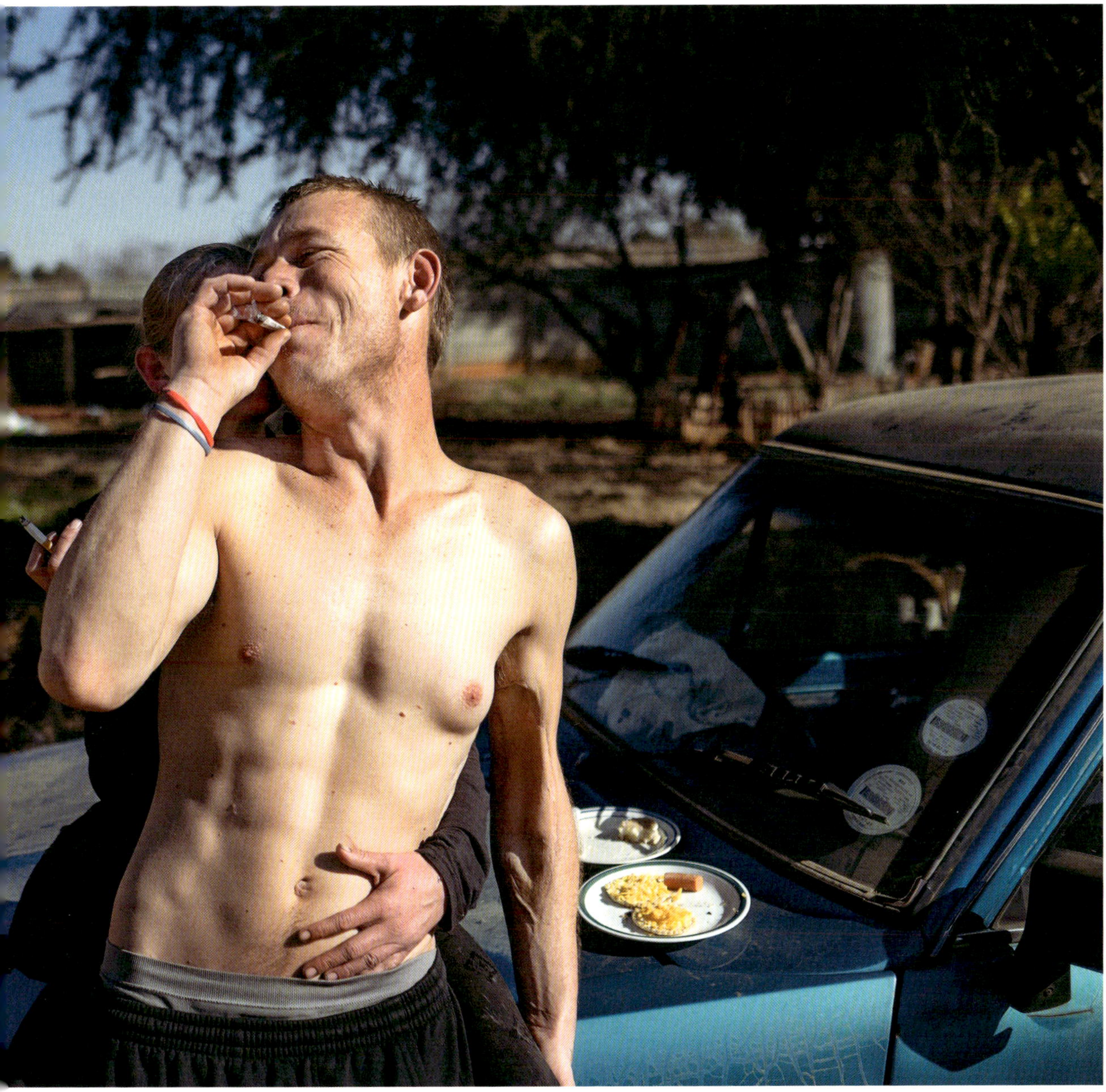

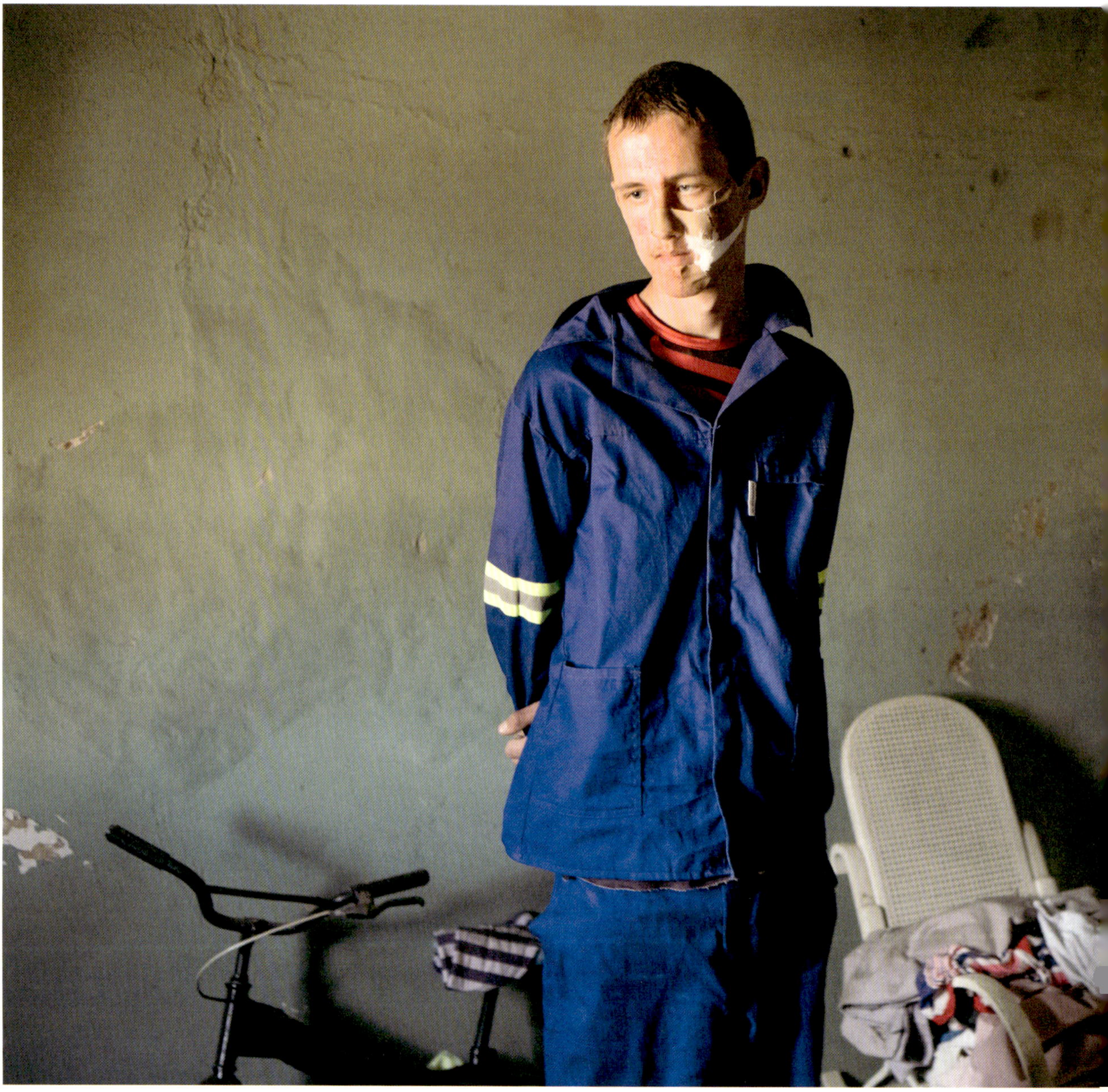

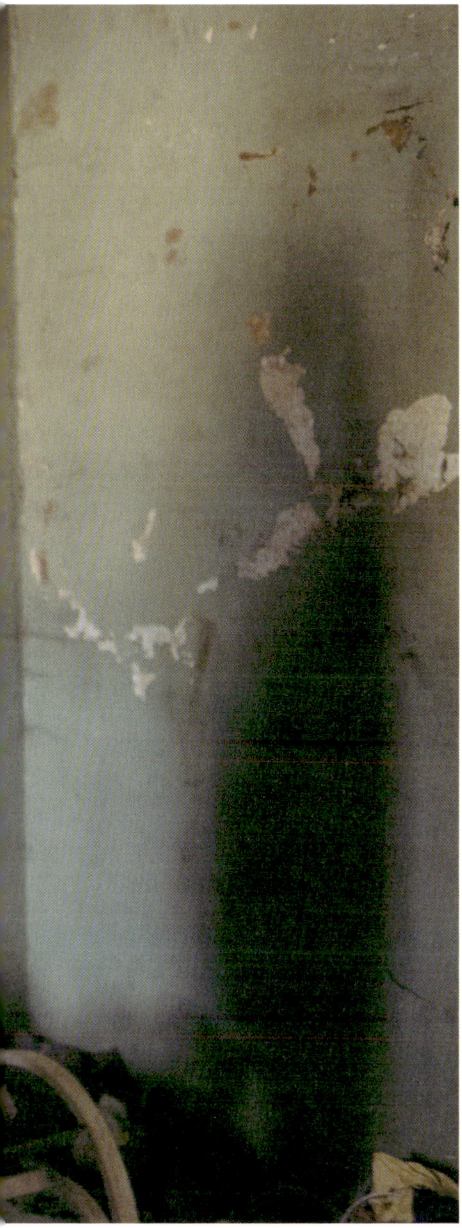

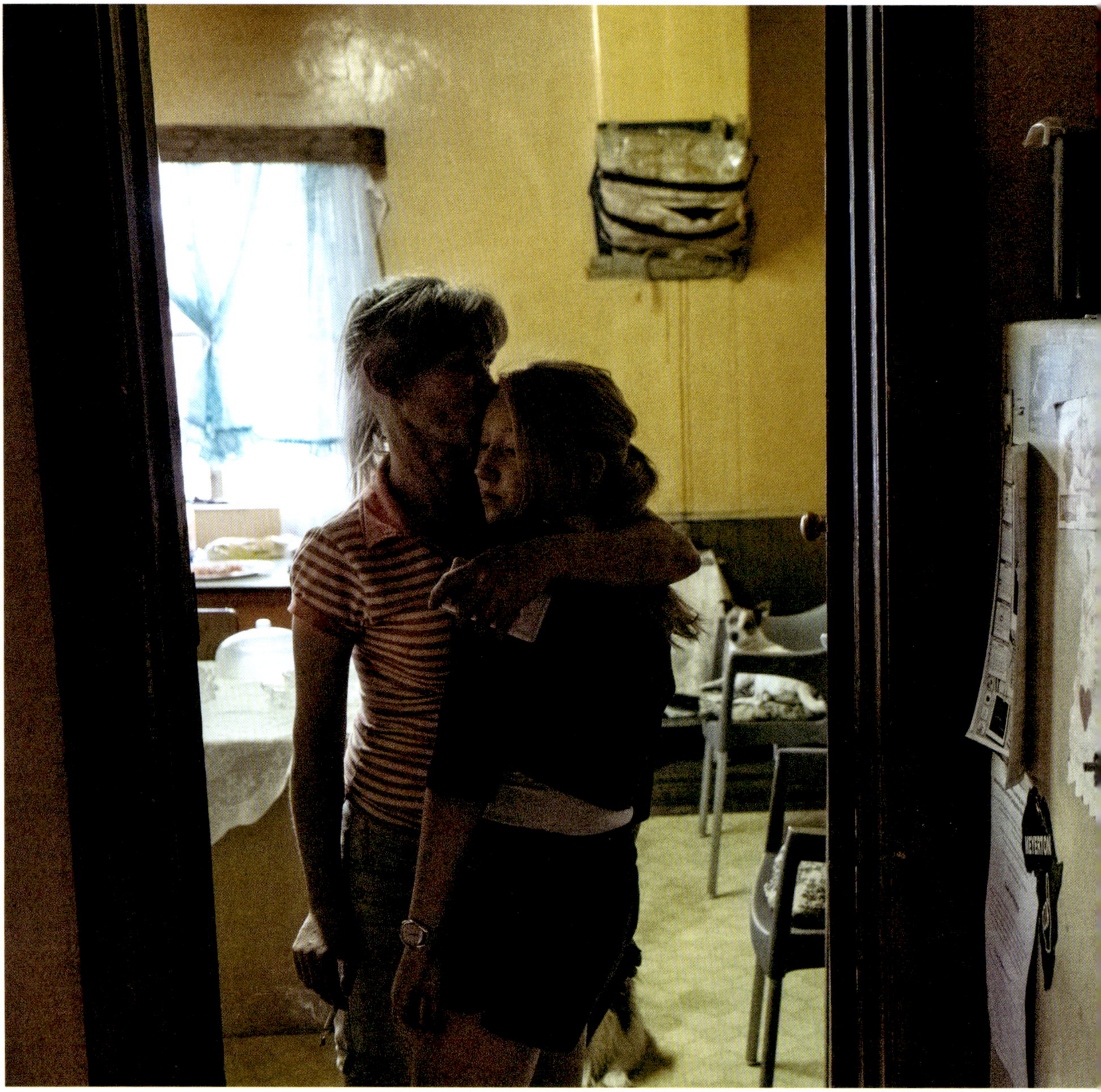

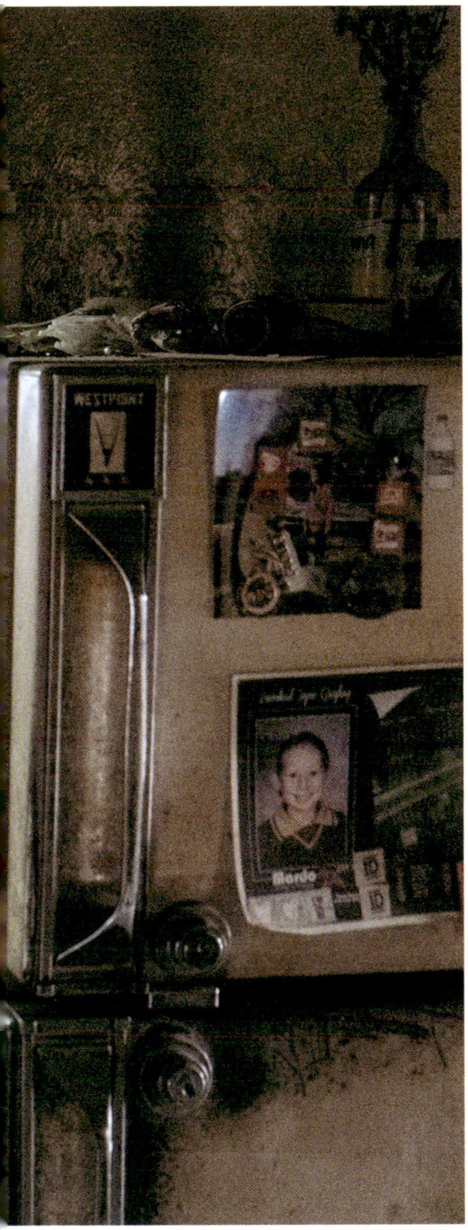
WESTPOINT

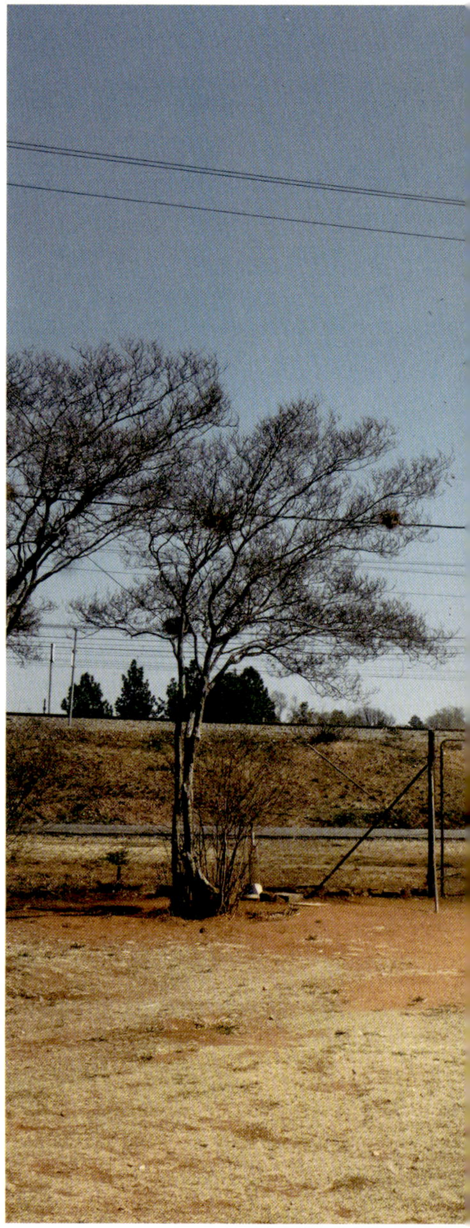

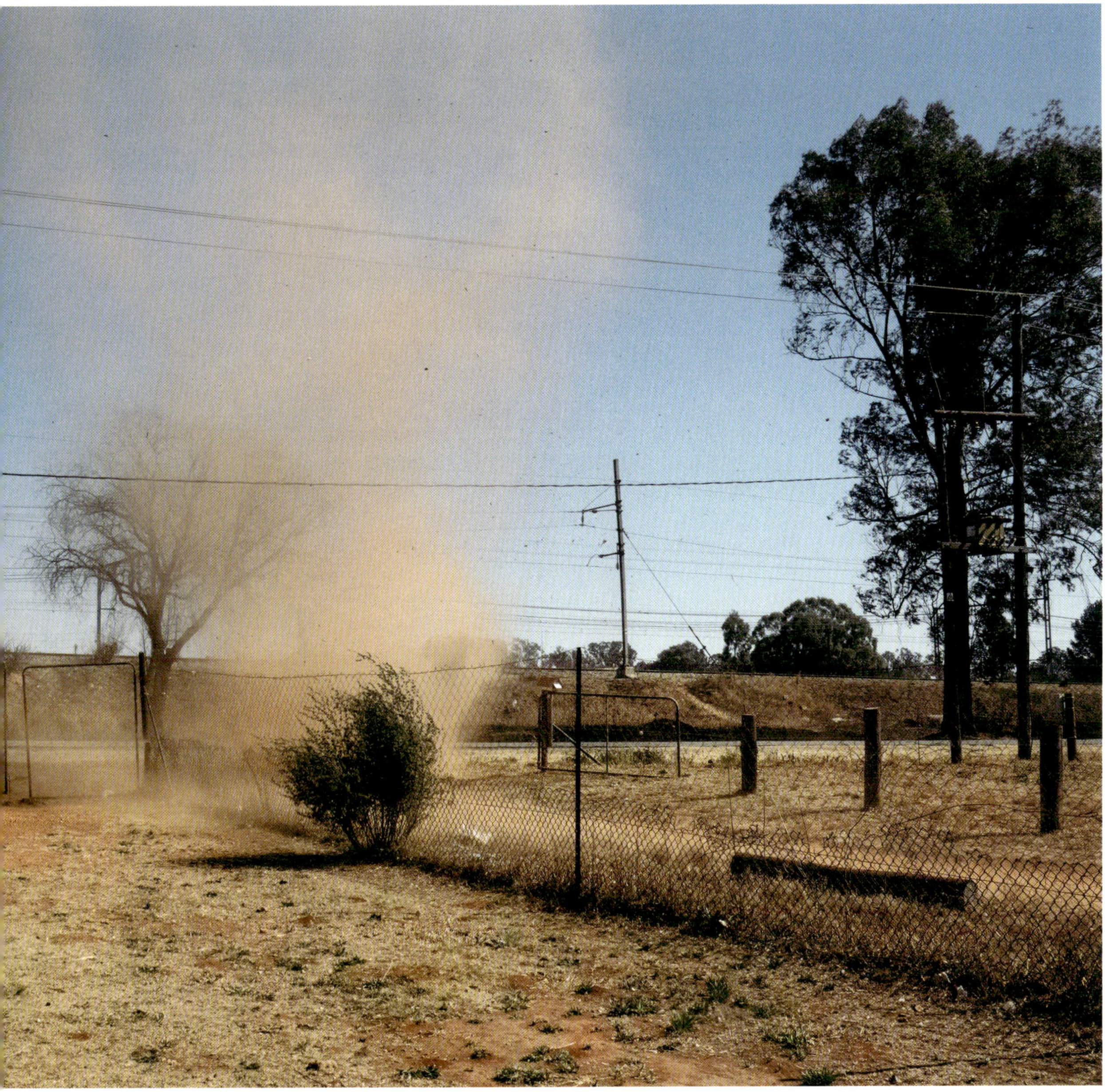

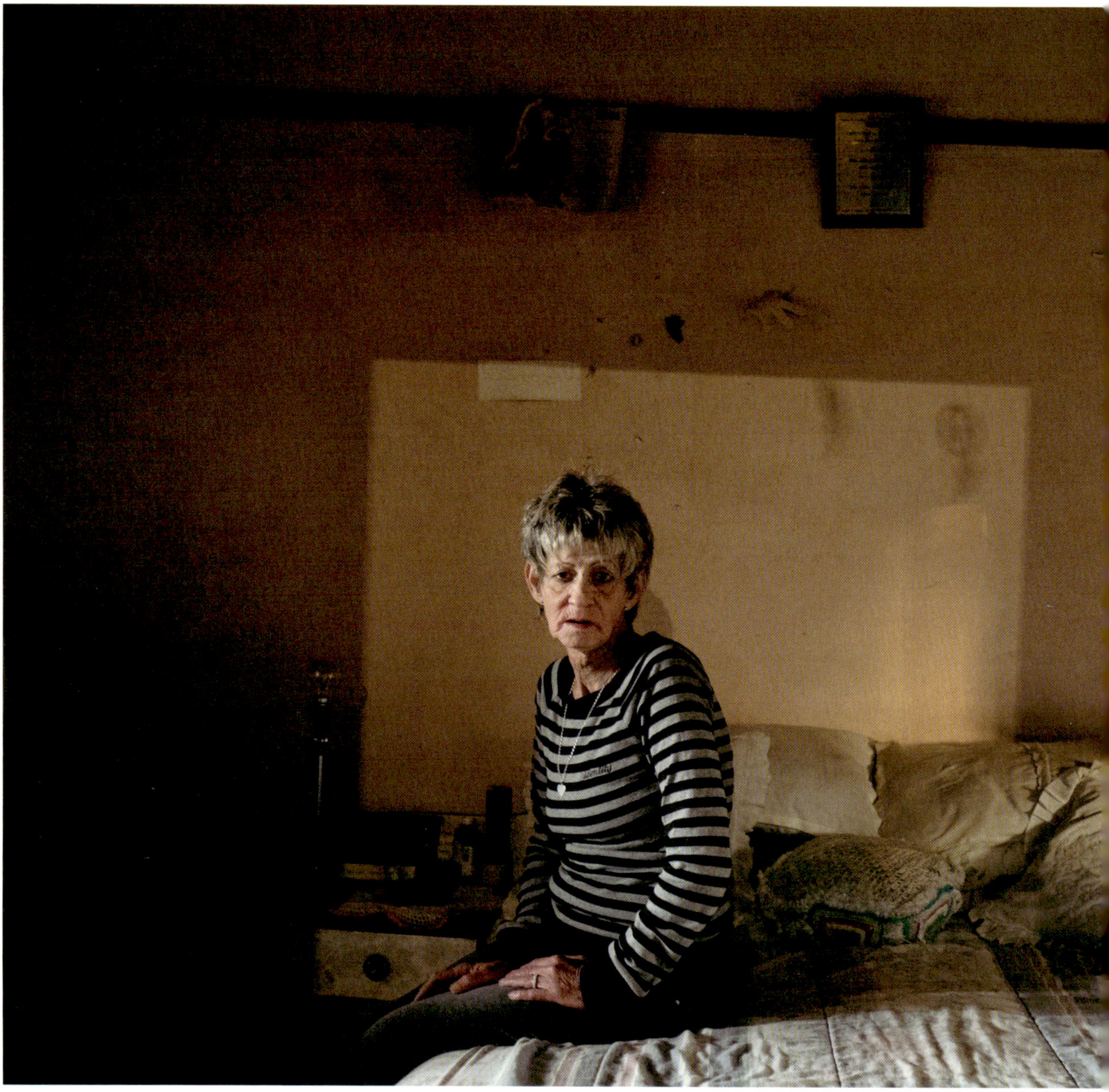

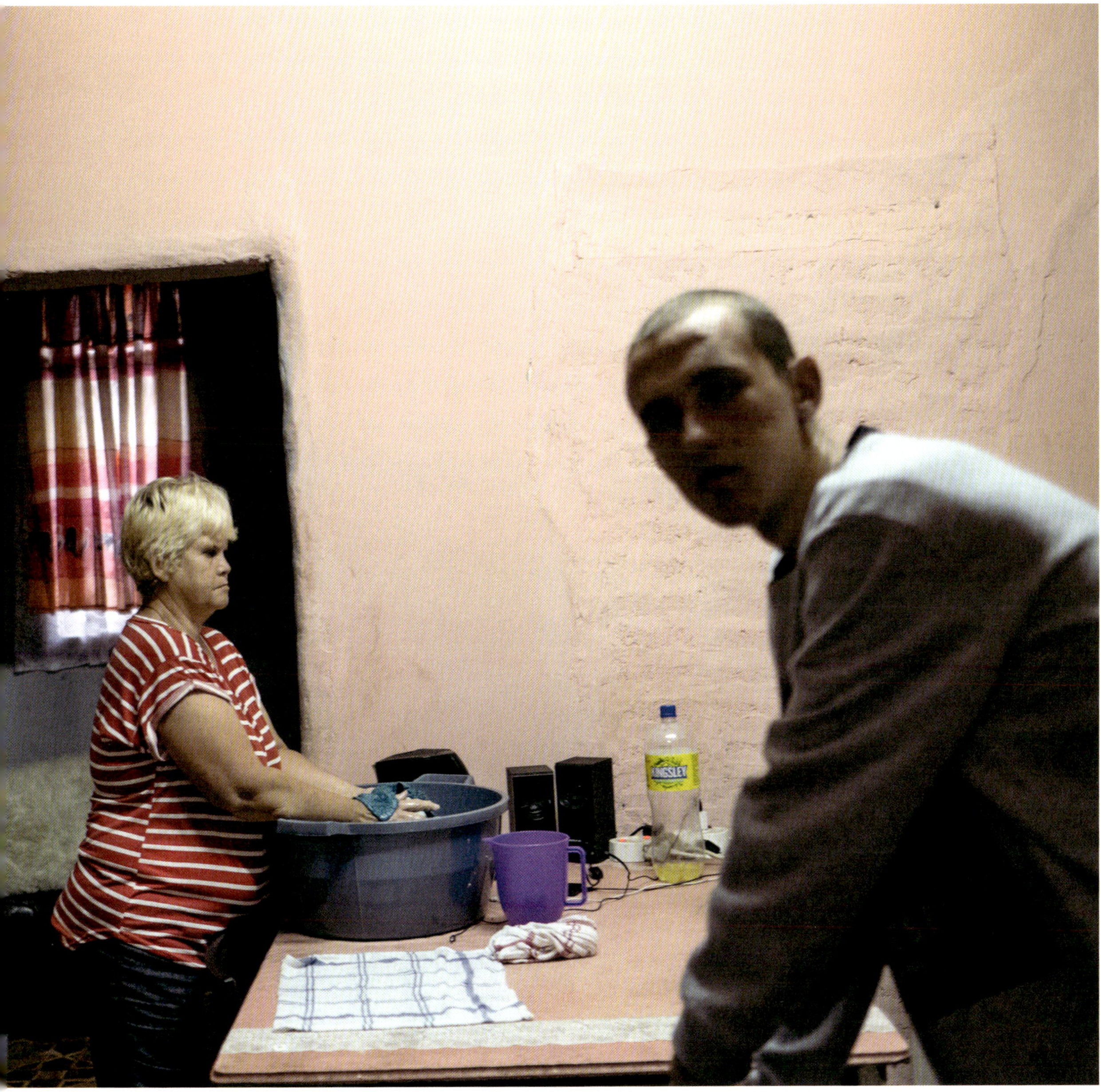

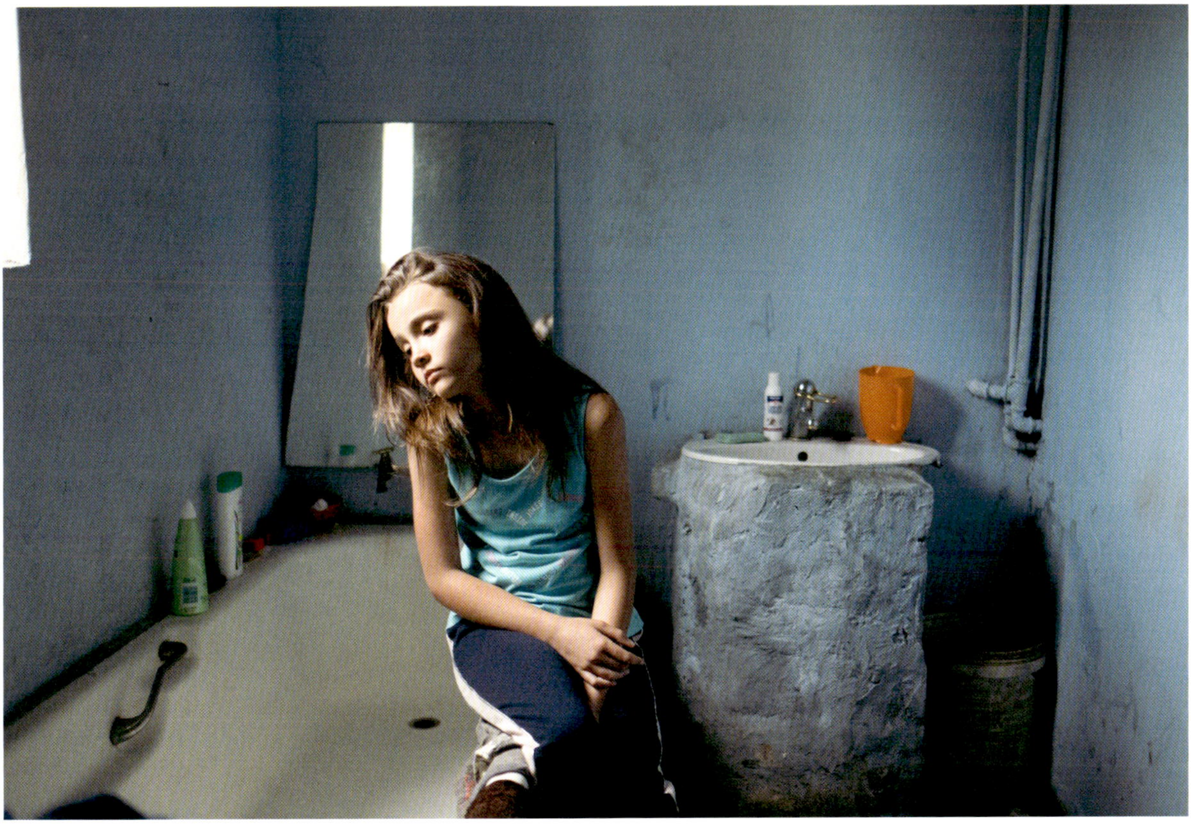

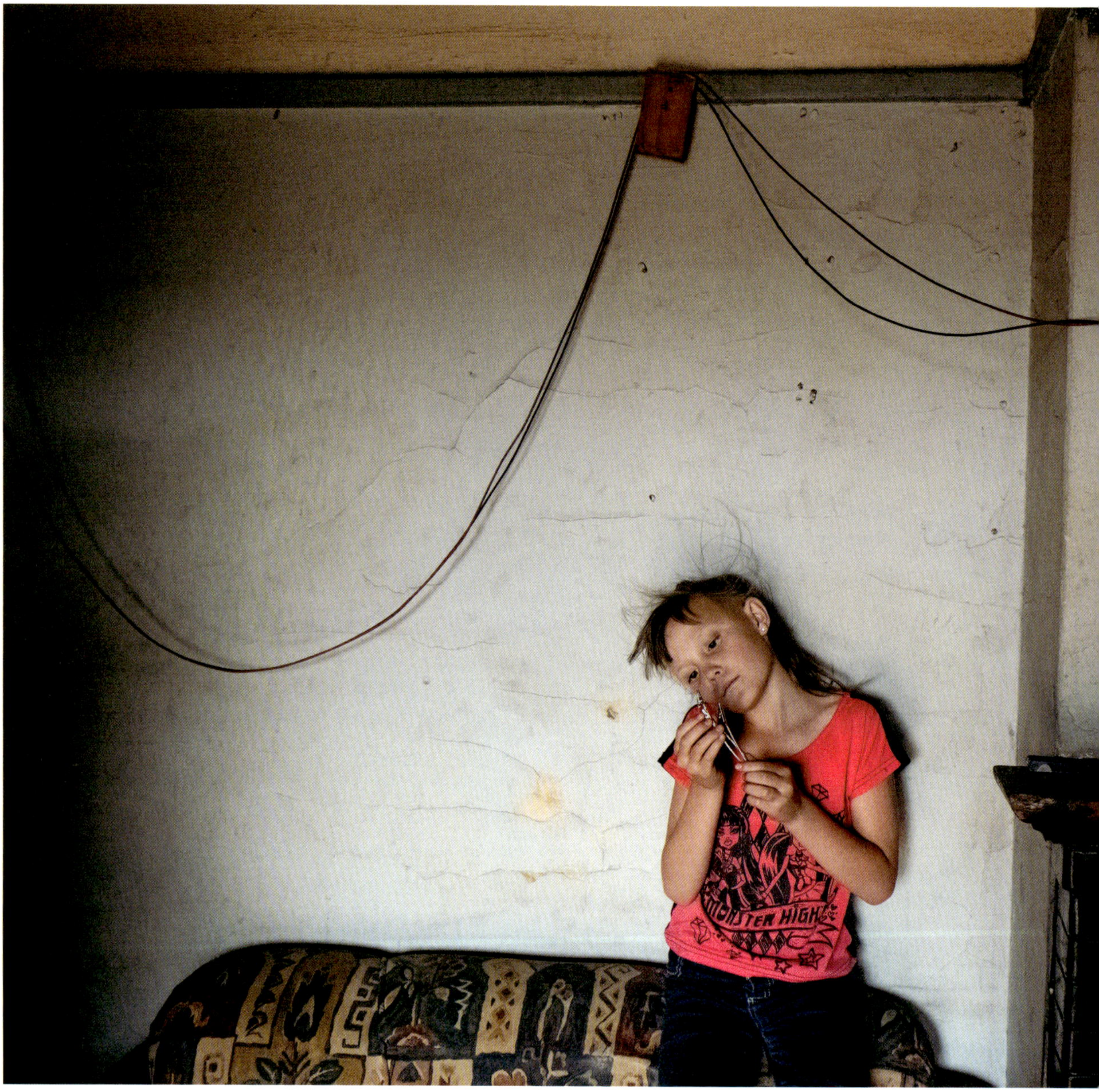
MONSTER HIGH

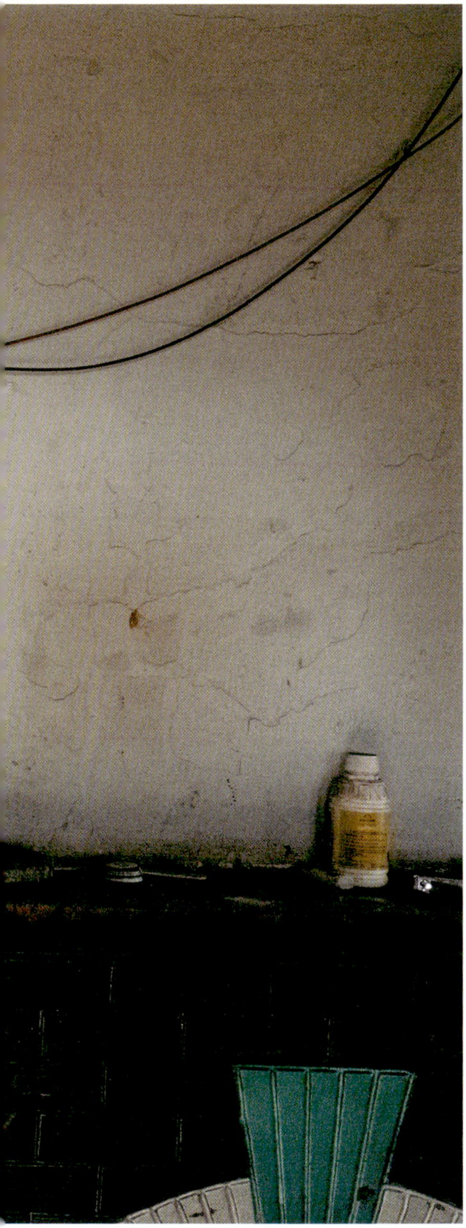

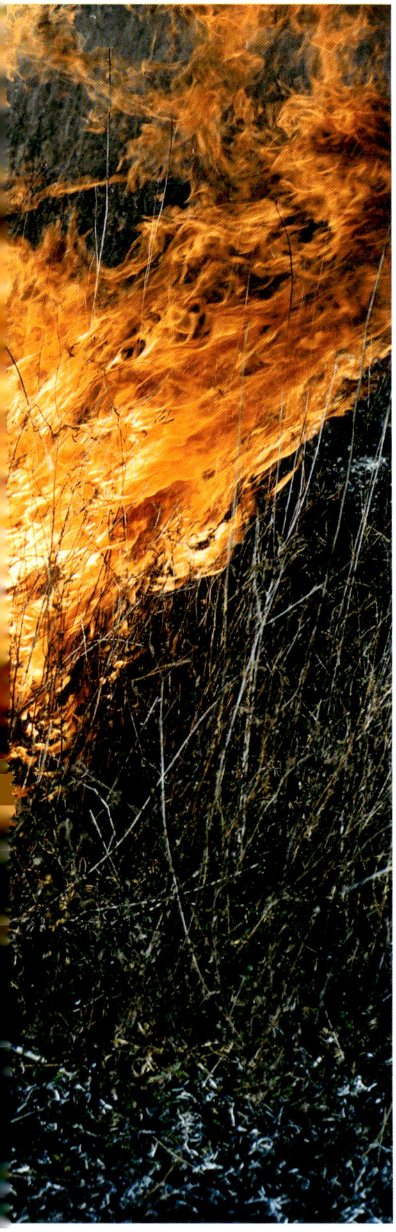

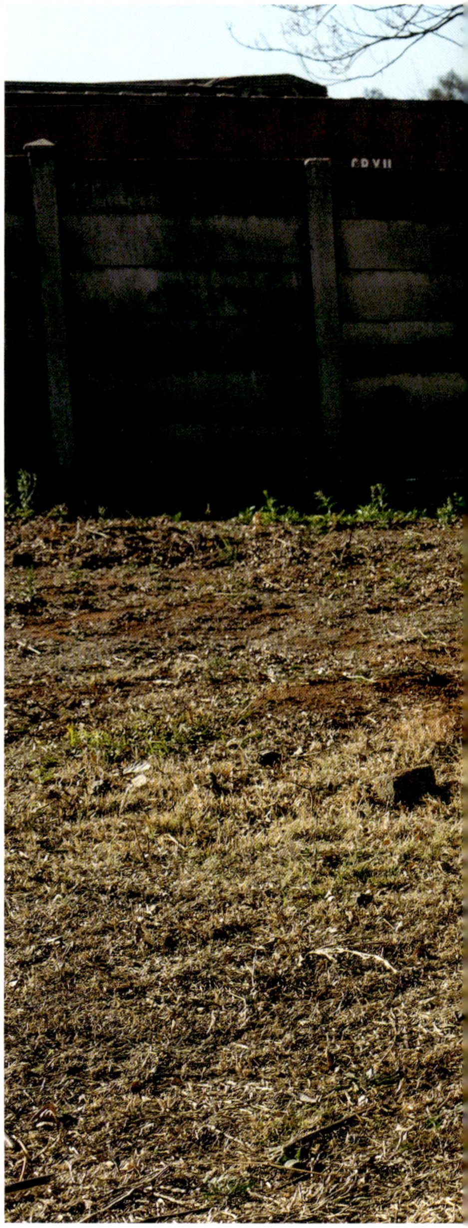

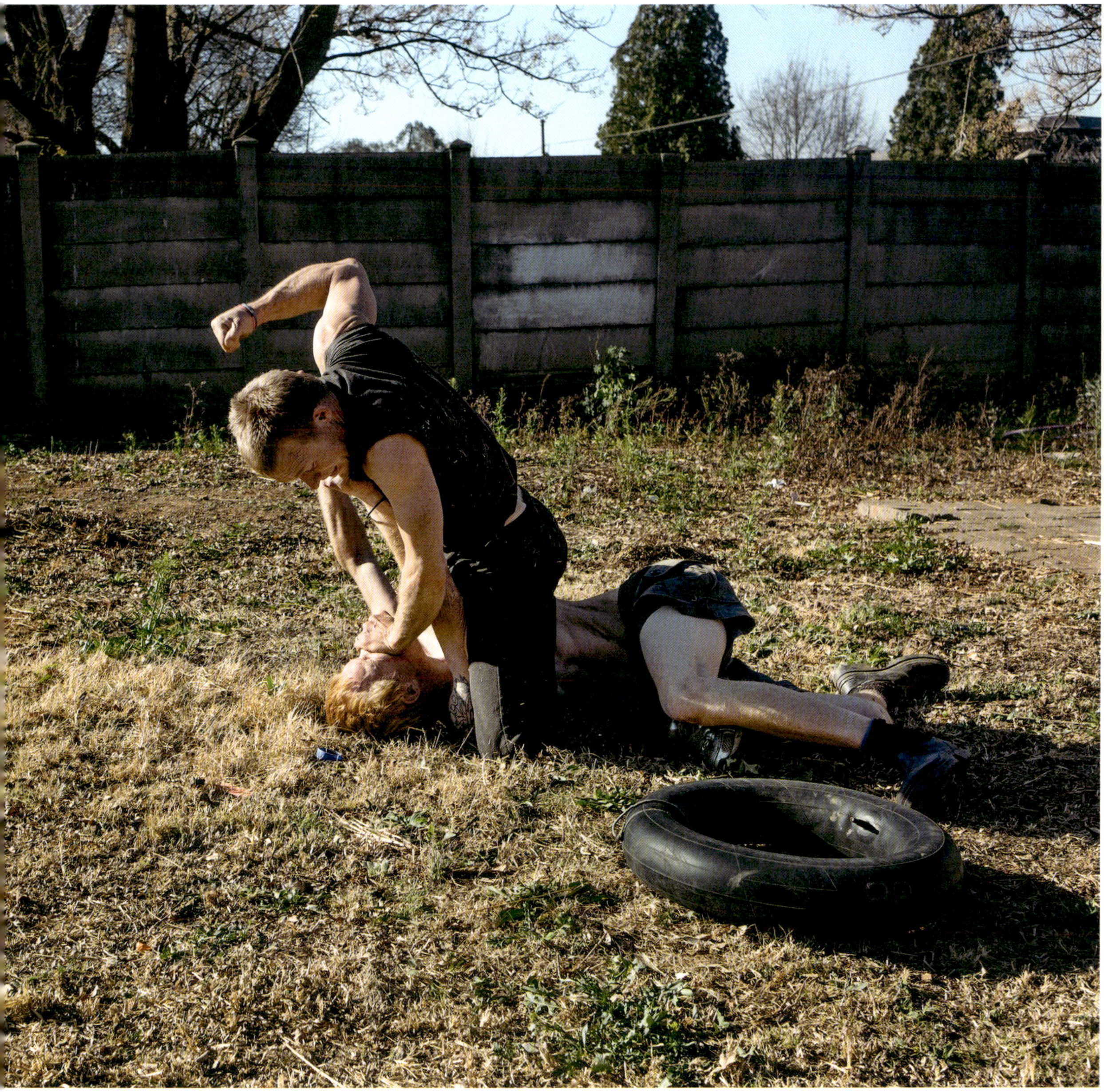

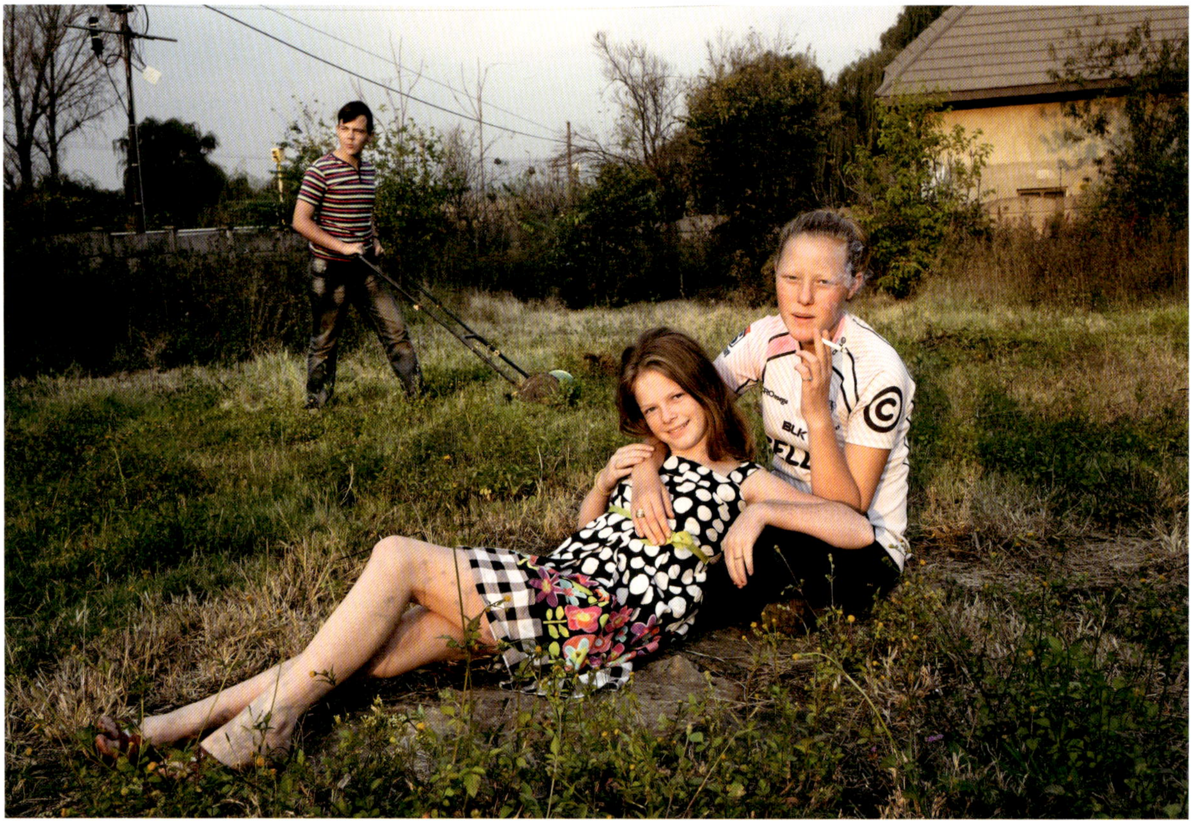

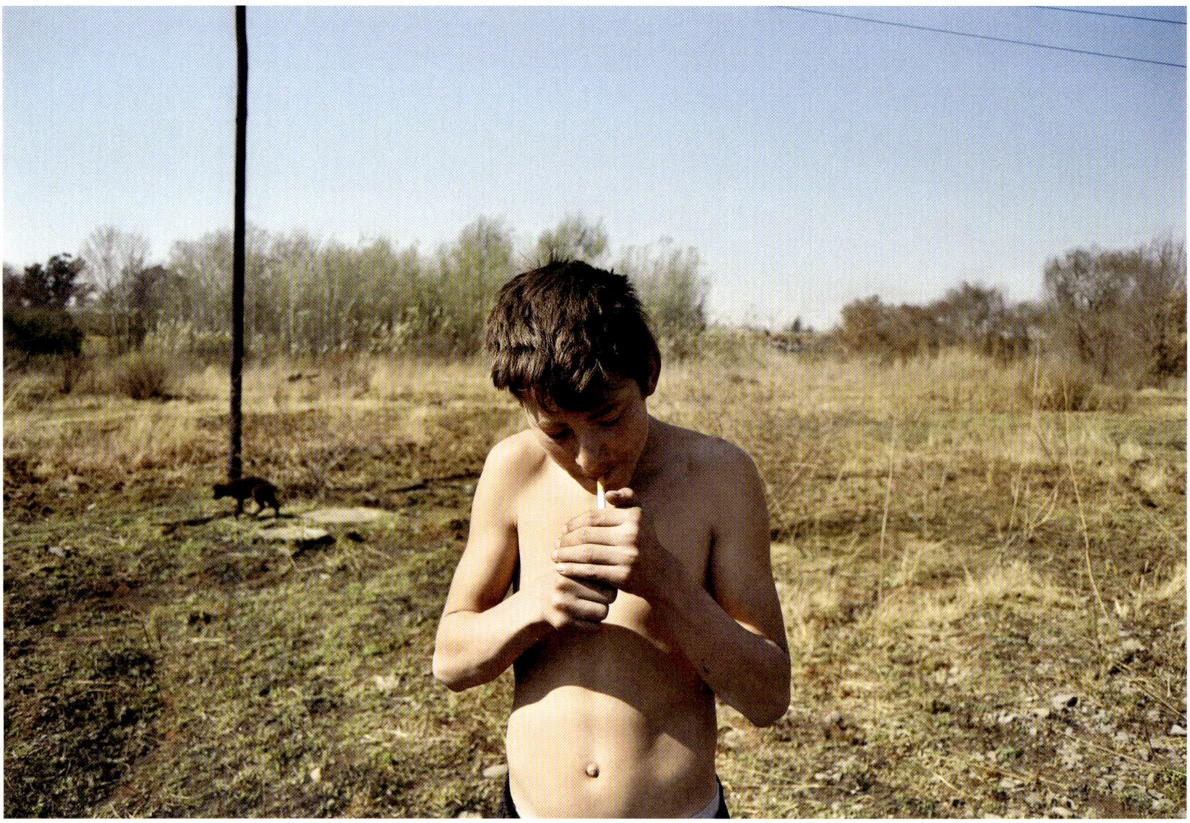

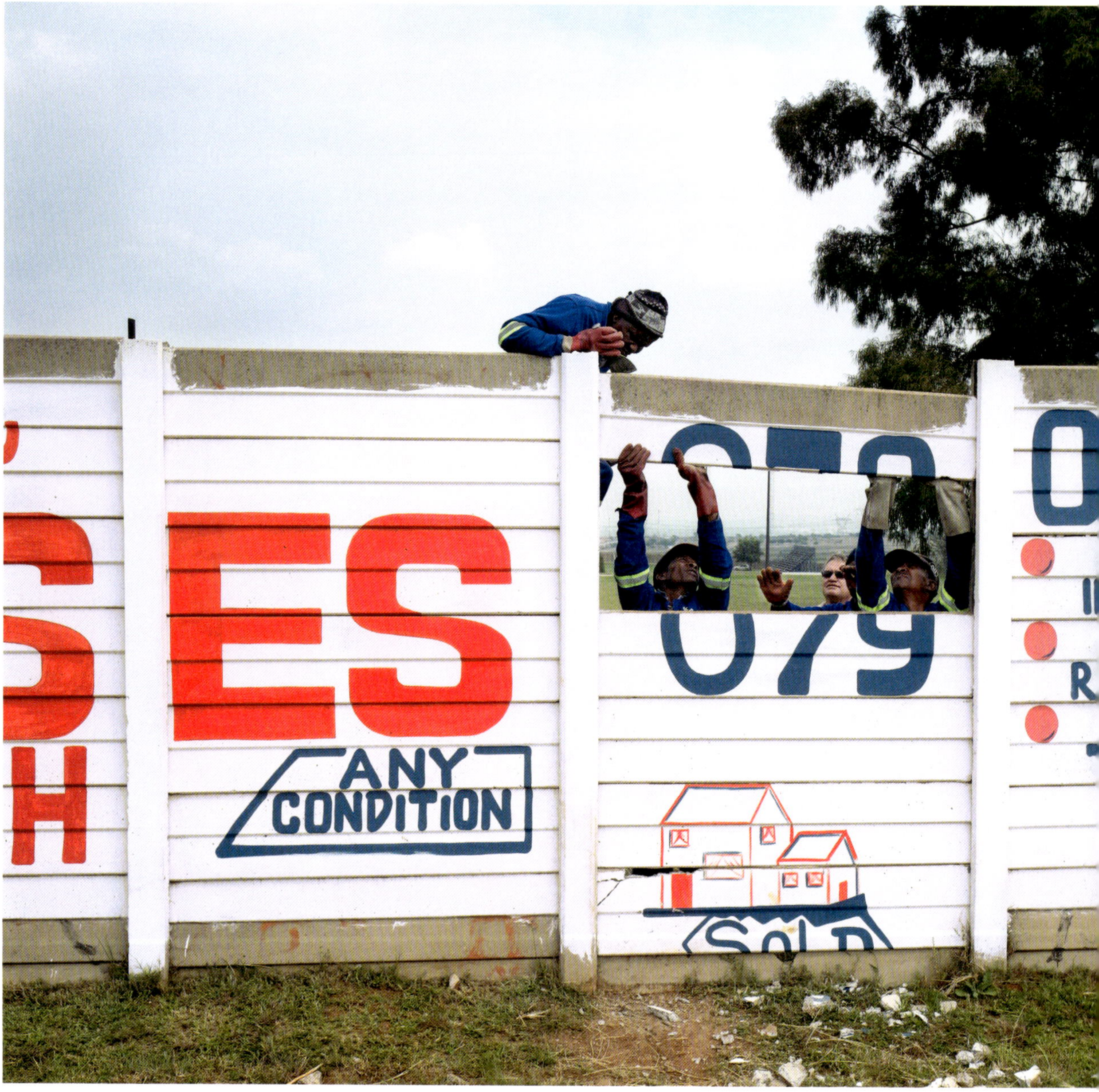
ES
ANY
CONDITION
079

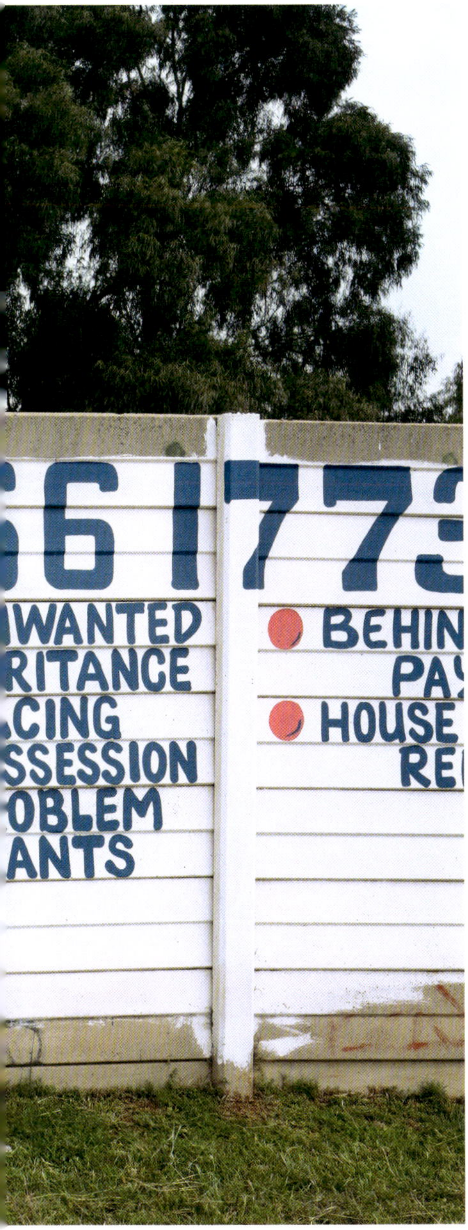

61773
WANTED
RITANCE
CING
SSESSION
OBLEM
ANTS
BEHIN
PA
HOUSE
RE

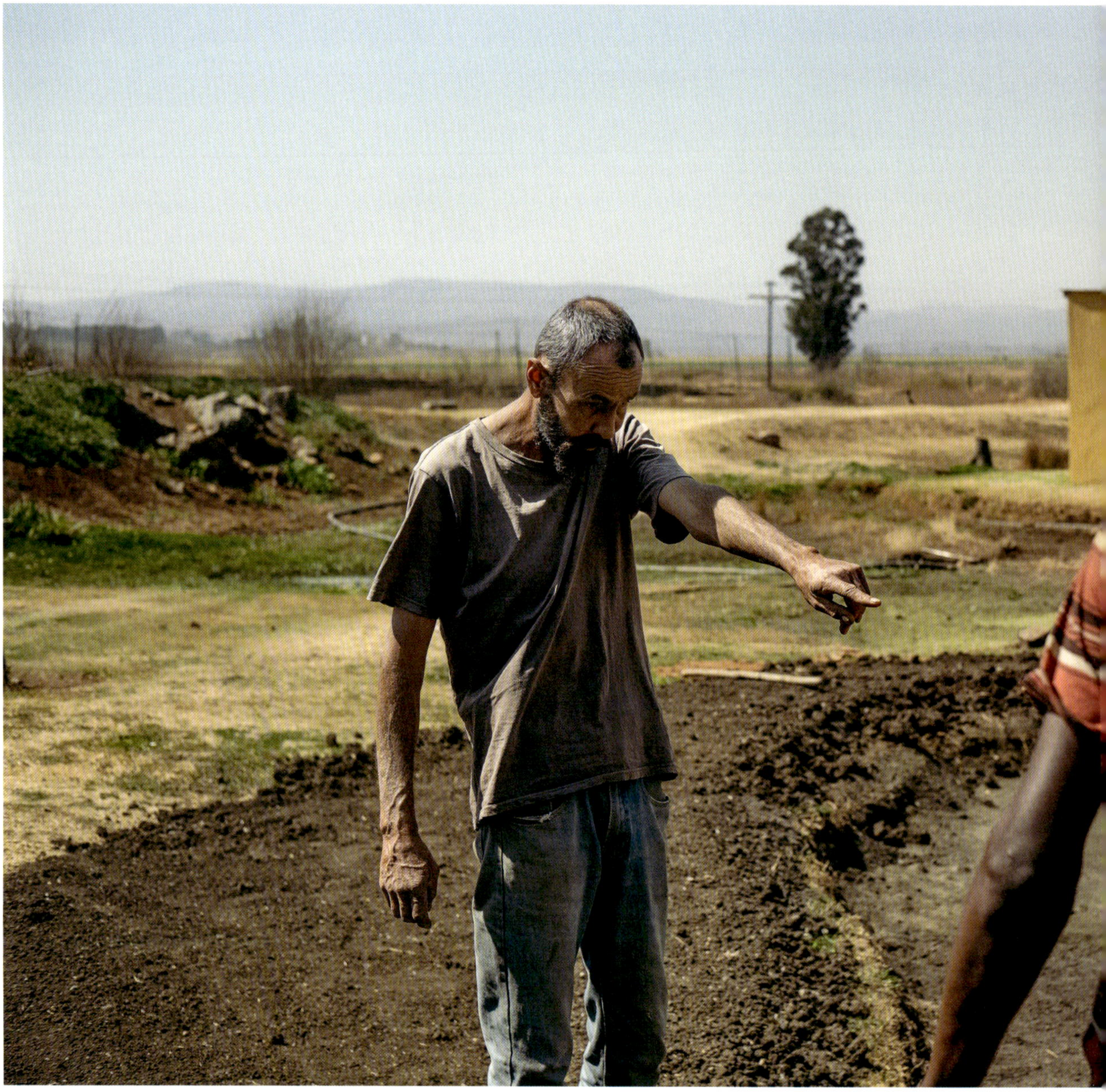

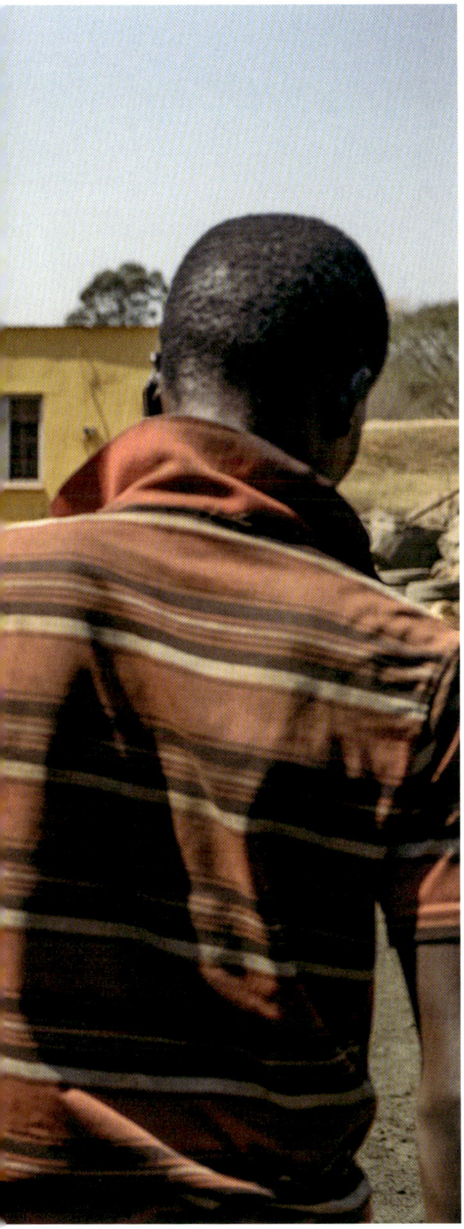

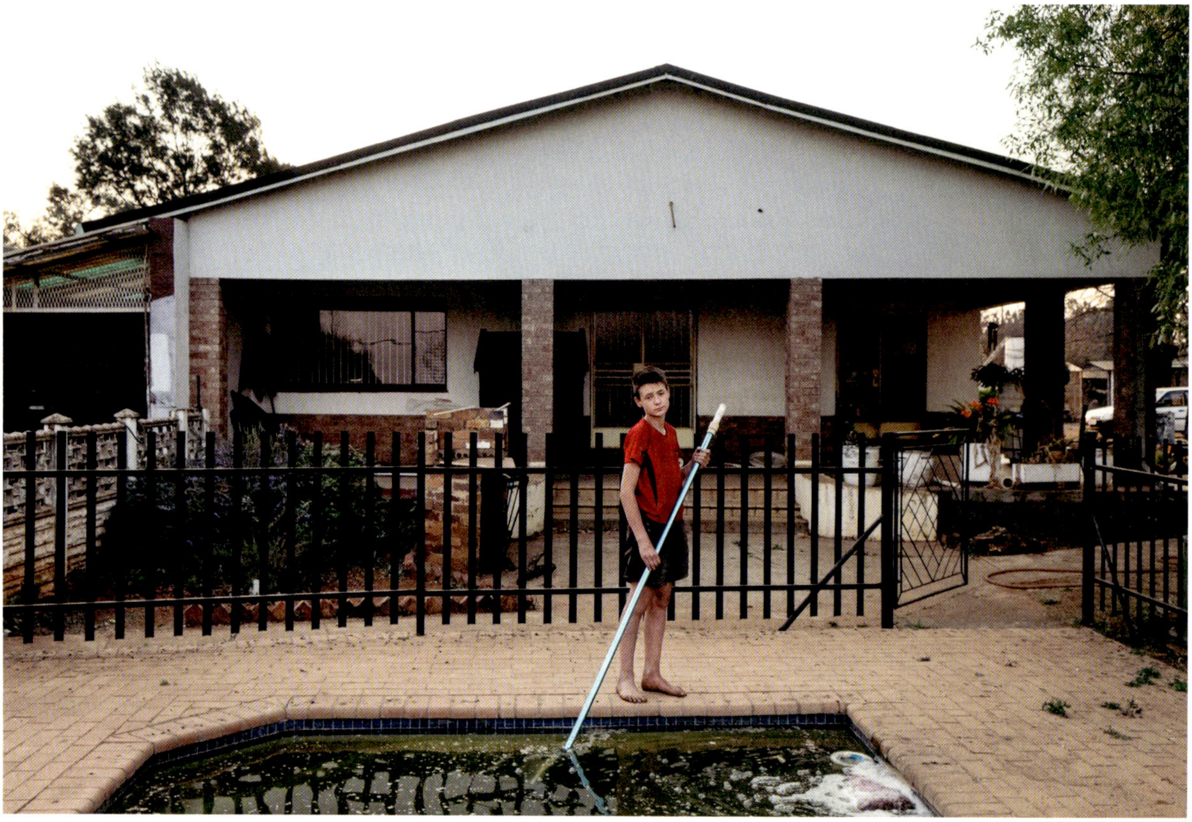

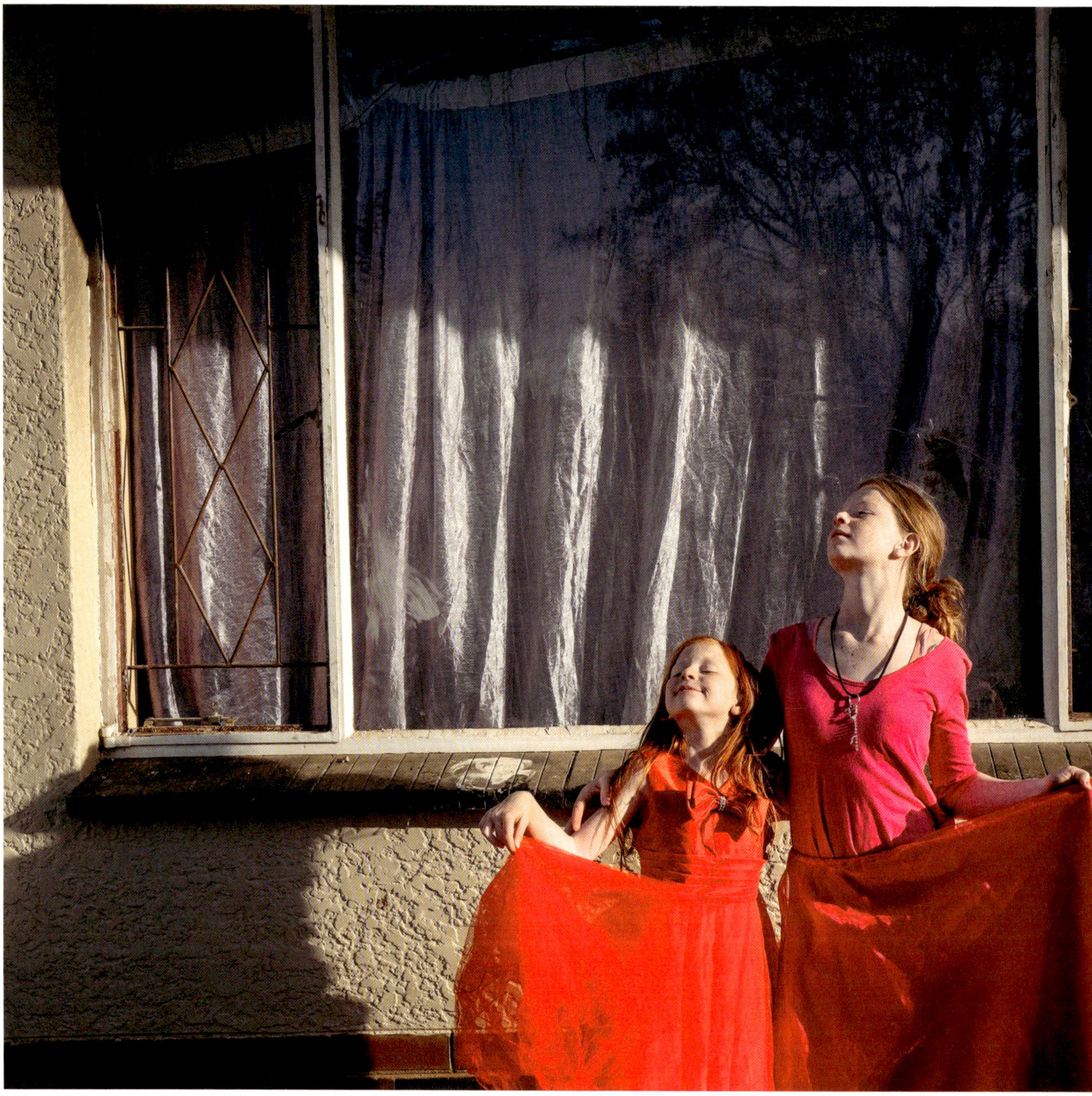

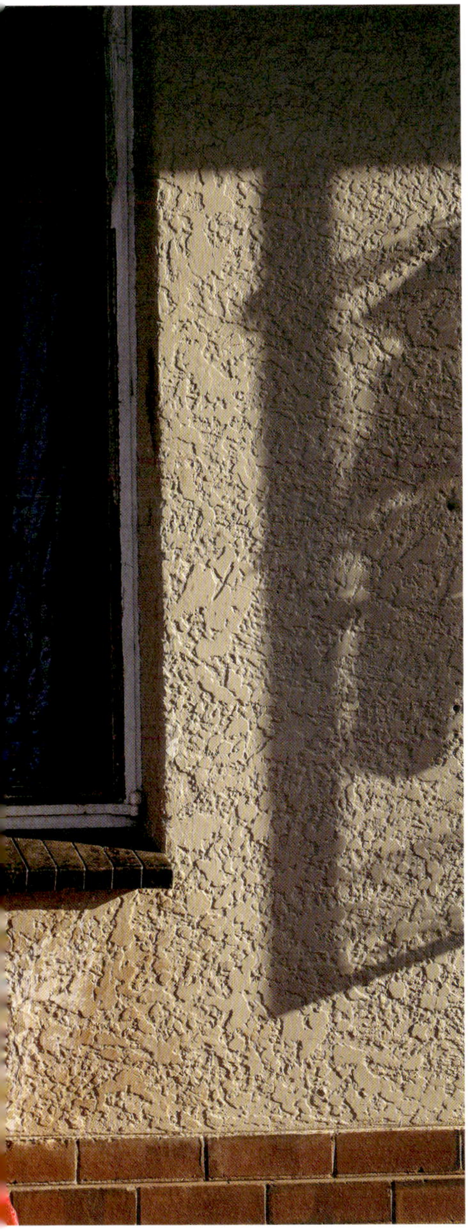

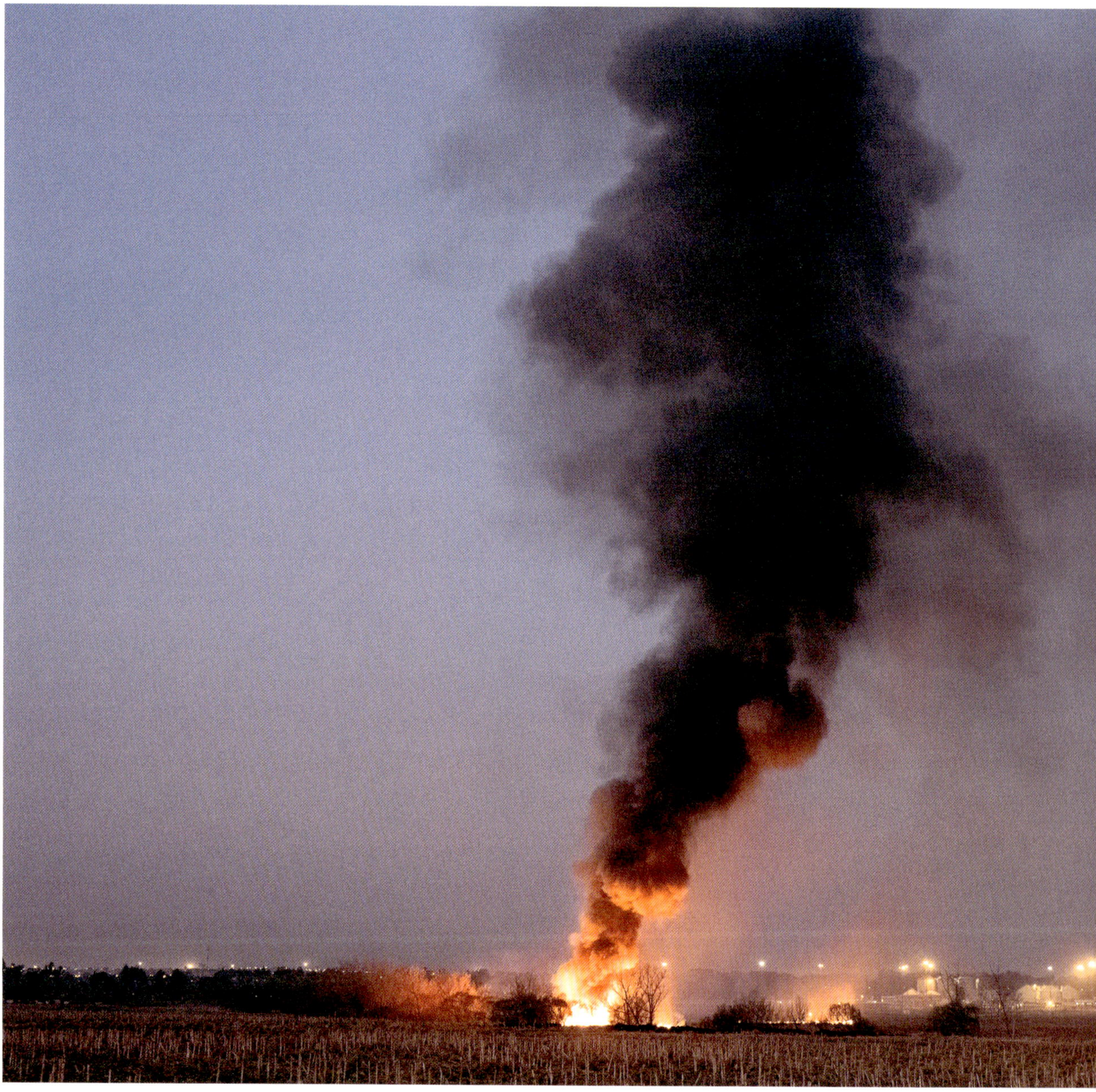

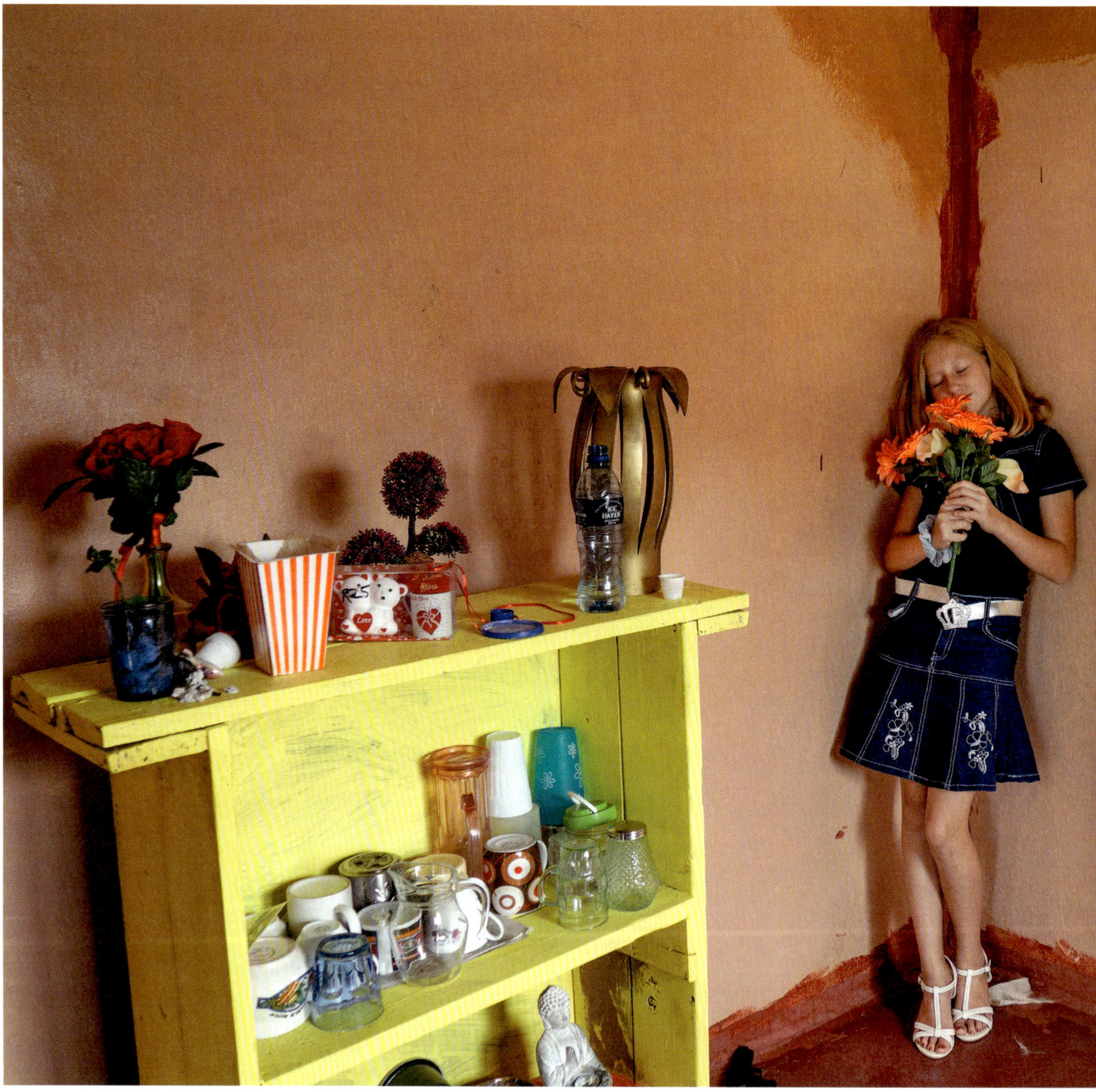

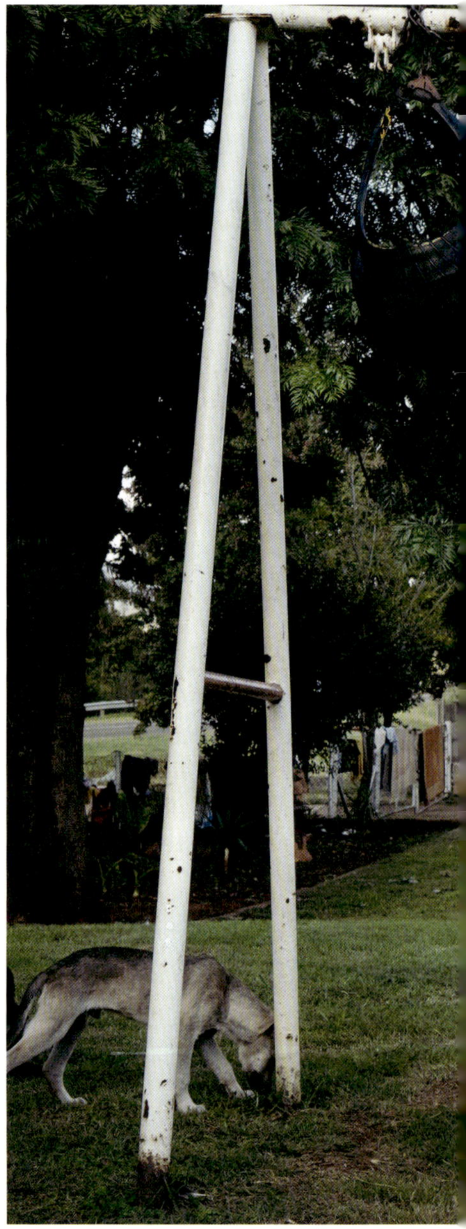

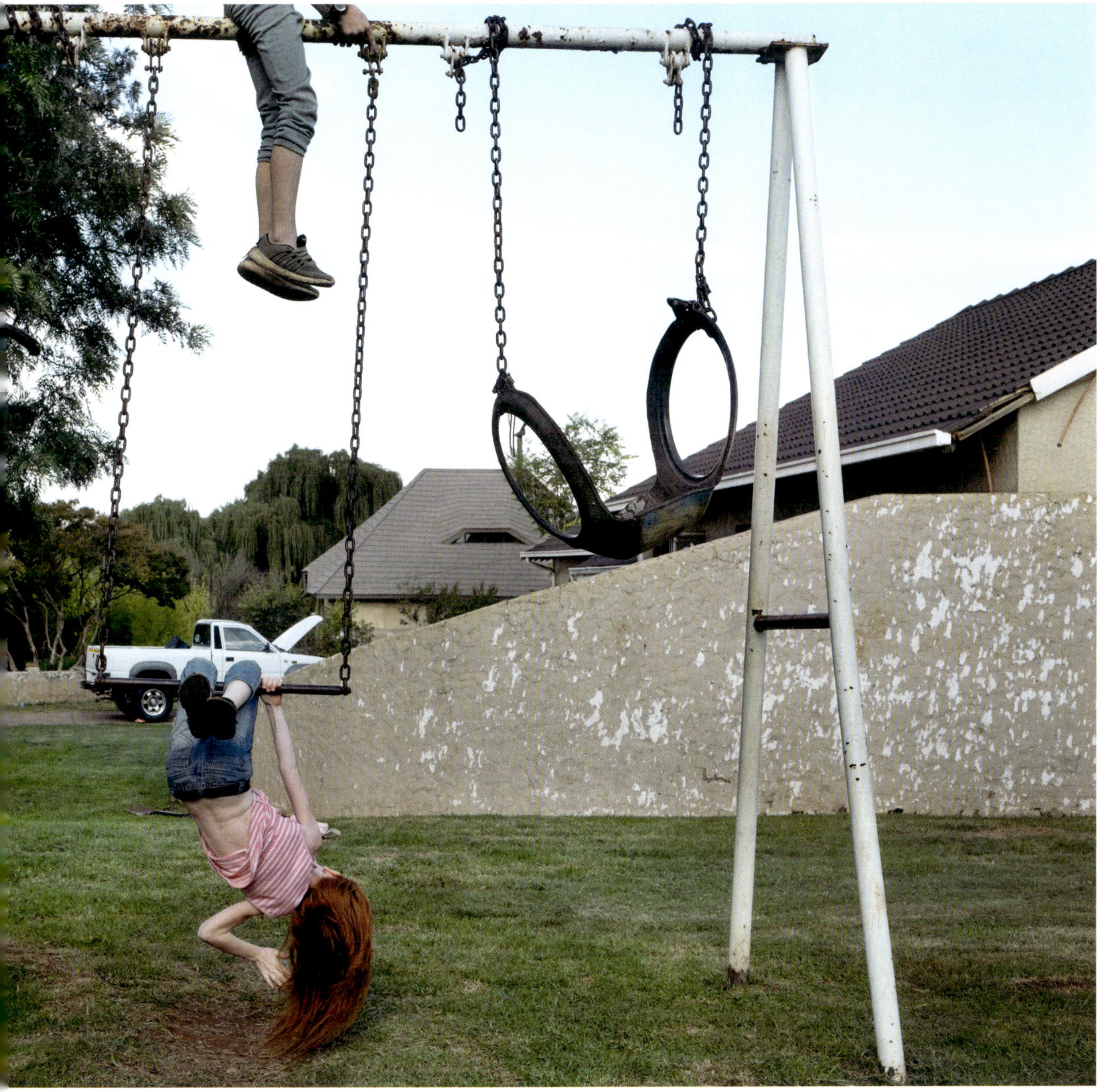

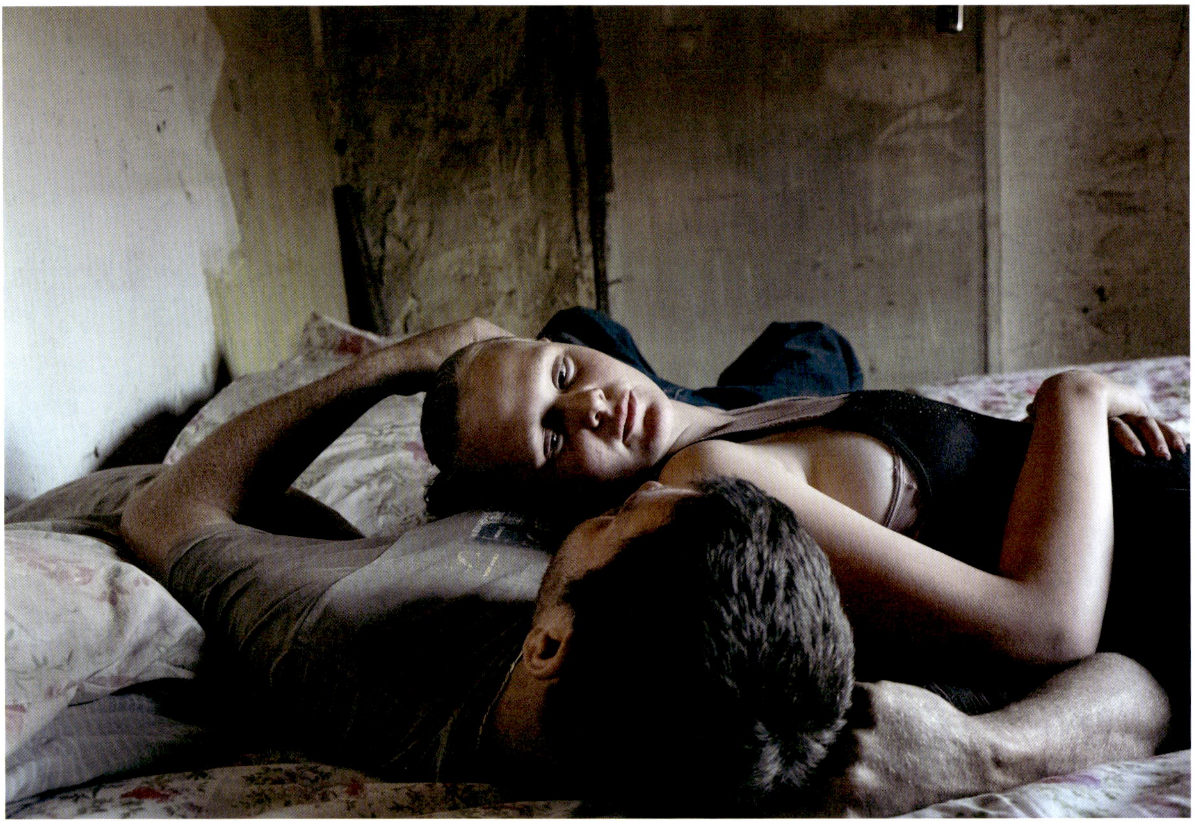

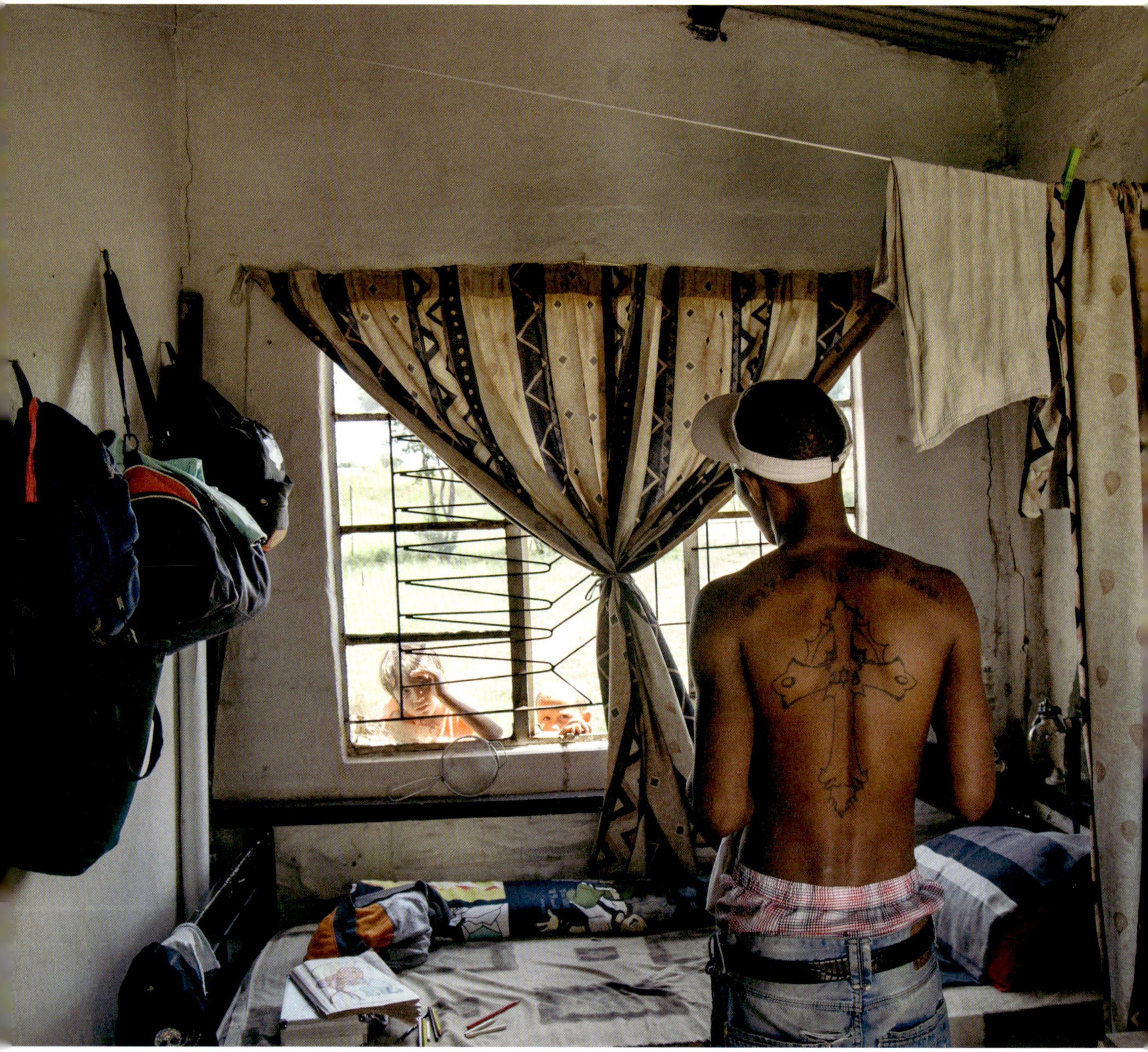

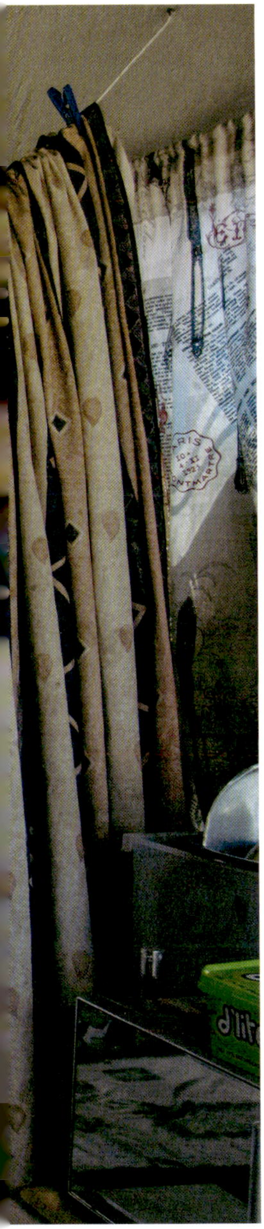

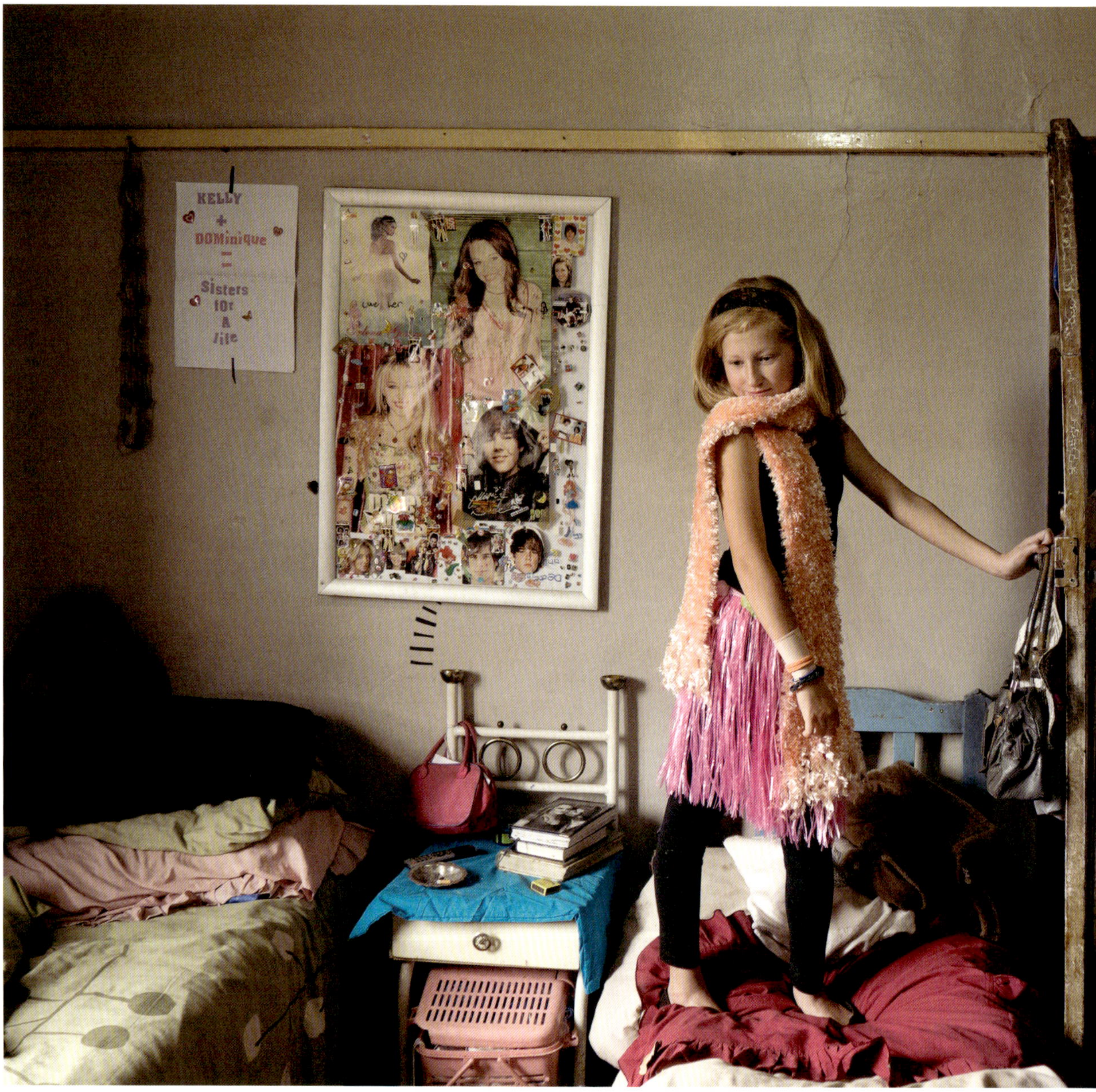
KELLY
+
DOMinique
=
Sisters
for
A
life

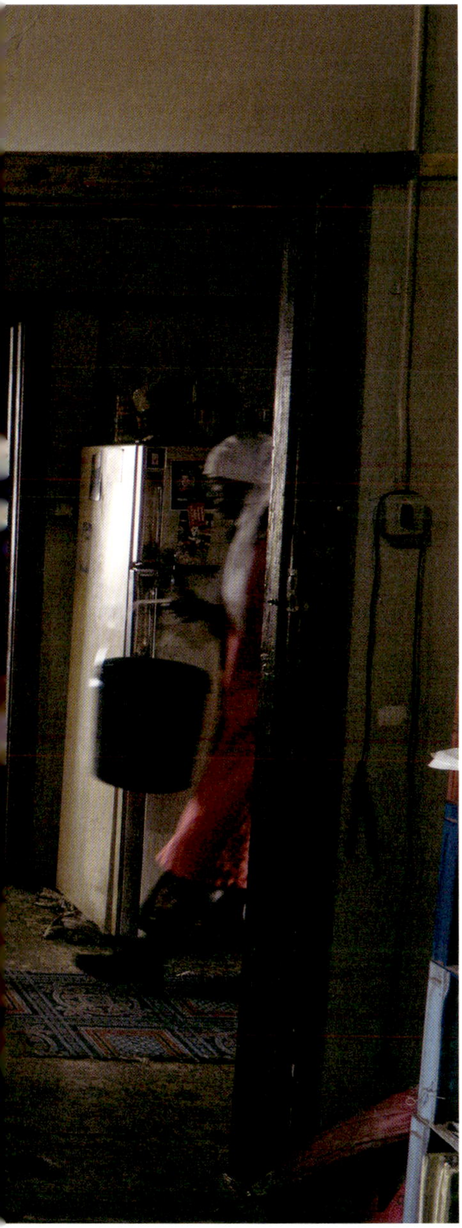

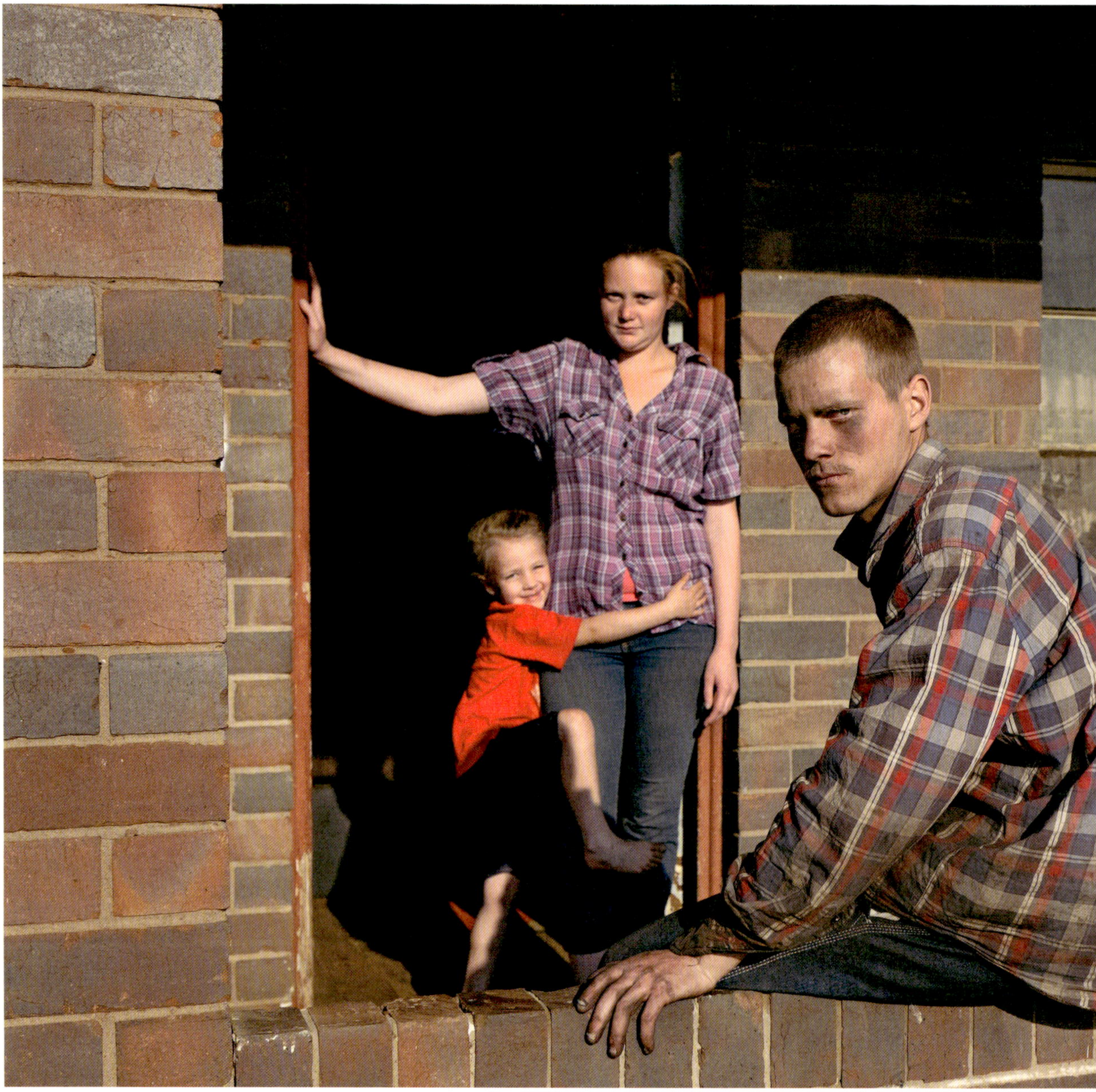

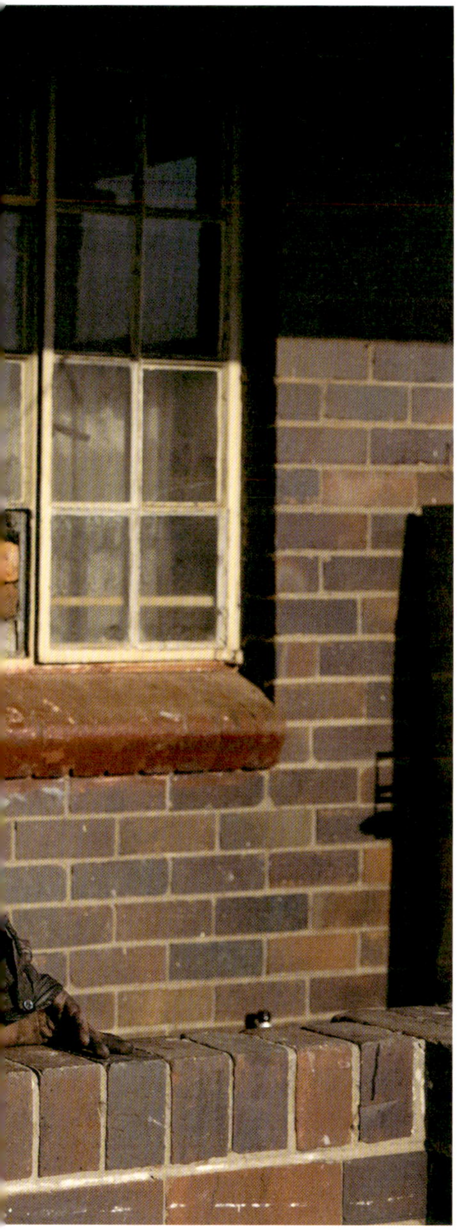

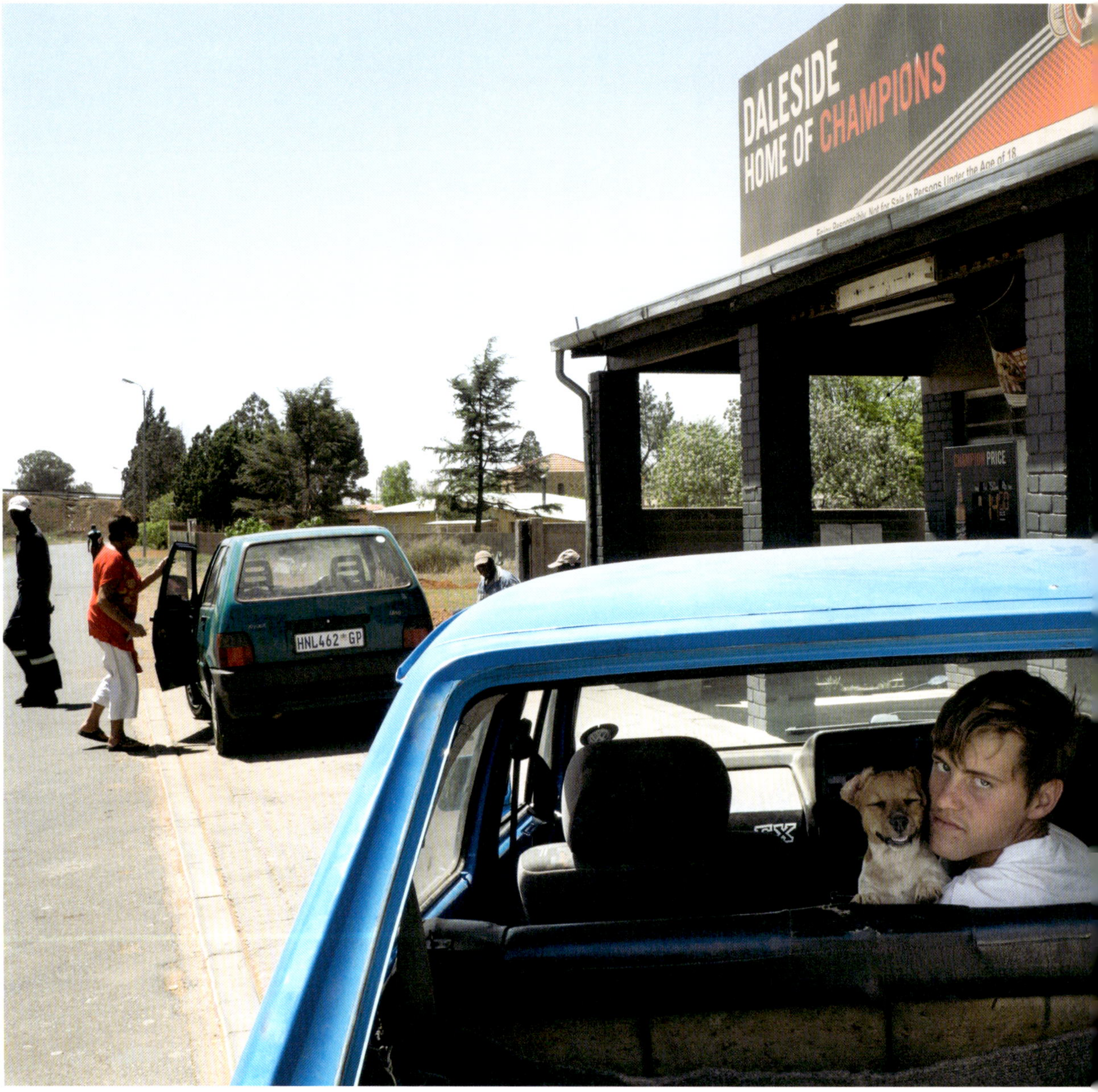
DALESIDE
HOME OF CHAMPIONS
HNL462 GP

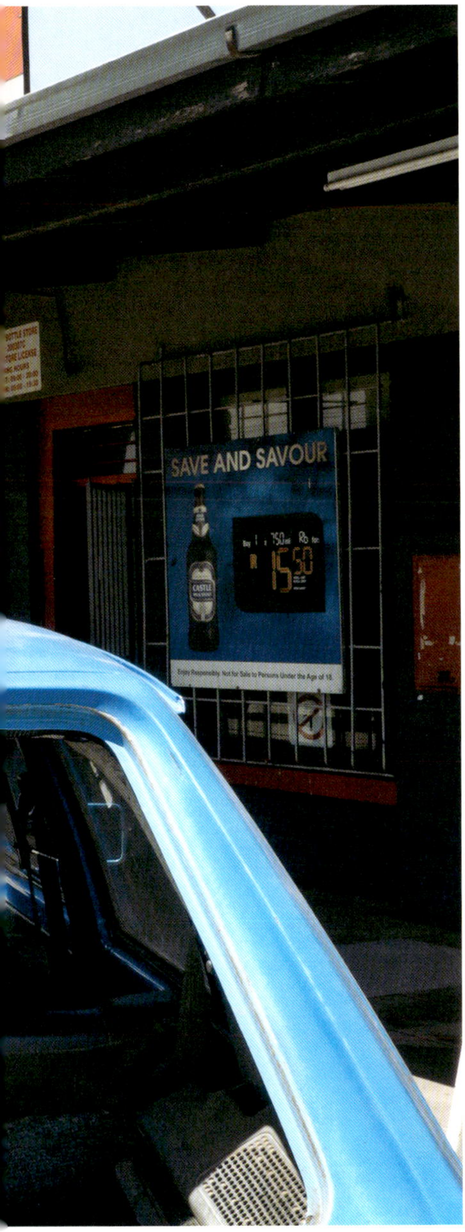
SAVE AND SAVOUR
CASTLE
R 15.50

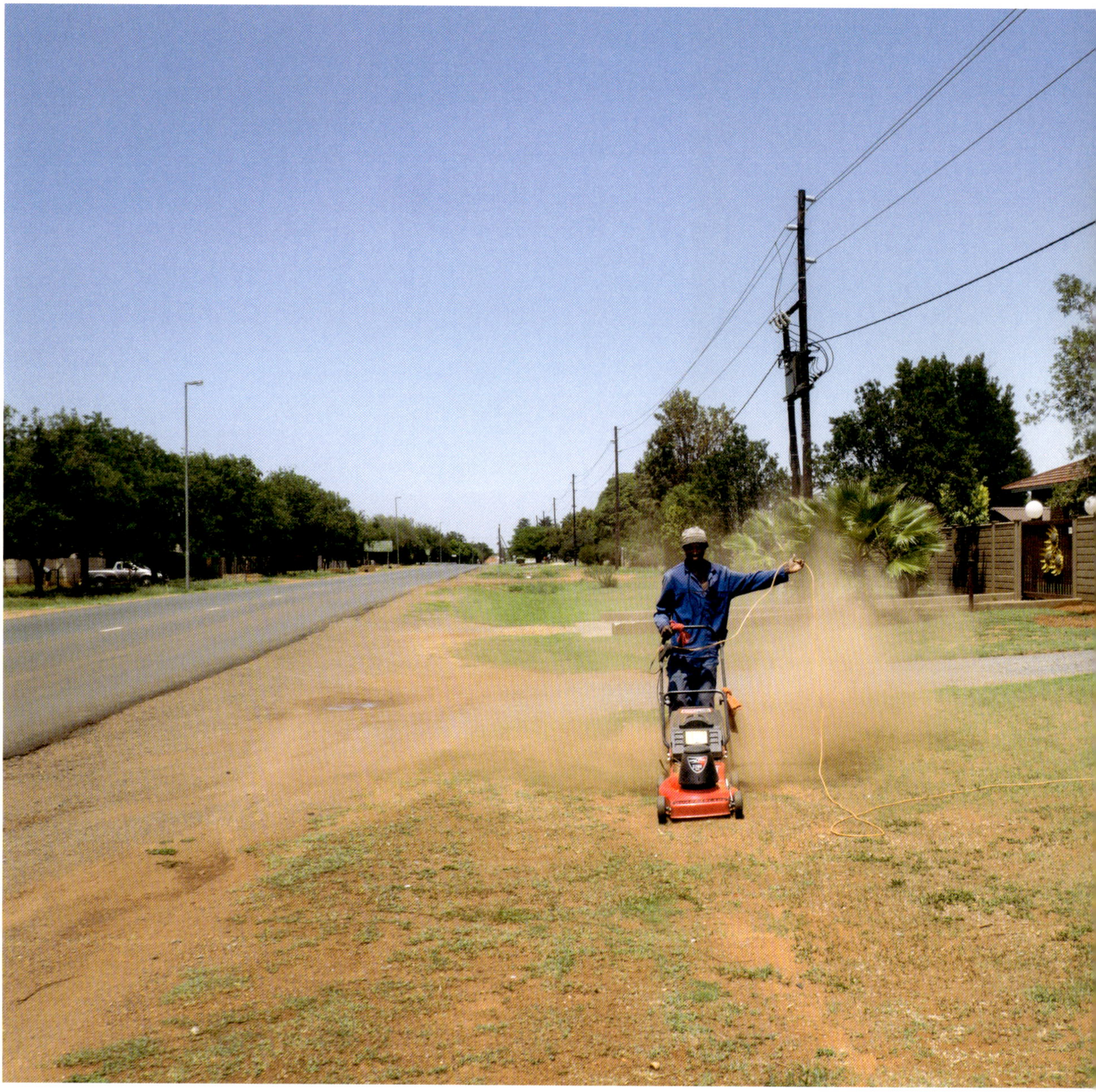

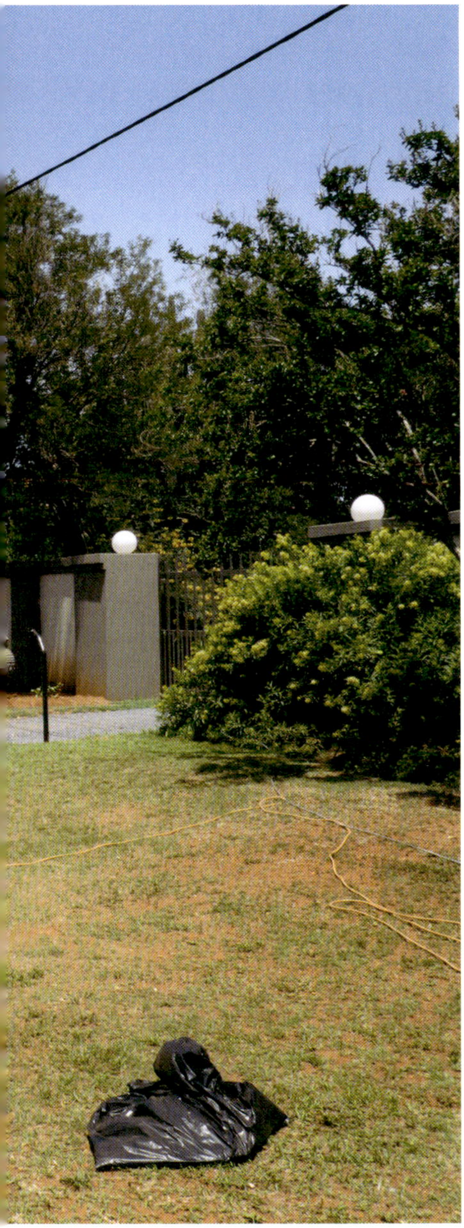

I first visited Daleside when my mother was employed there as a domestic worker. At the time, the white-dominated area seemed like an isolated place, a ghost town. It is a place I have always had unresolved issues with and a curiosity about since I first visited. While growing up, the community was a place I always felt took so much from me—mainly my mother—who had to live there for her line of work. When I was a young boy and went to visit her, I was denied entrance at what to me felt like some kind of paradise. Going back there to photograph was a way for me to confront these feelings, and in doing so, I realised it was not what I expected it to be.

Daleside is a community with all the systems that exist in any other. The people who live there, work in the mines or farms. It's almost as if the countryside has shifted into an urban environment. My work there focuses on the residents' intimate and personal spaces and—as my first project outside the townships—it has challenged me to leave my comfort zone.

While photographing in Daleside, I have to constantly be careful of how I approach people and their personal spaces. It takes a lot of energy and patience to get into these spaces and for people to trust me. I often come up with strategies that help me develop some trust—whether it's attending a church service or carrying with me a photo album with the photographs I was making—to show I am not there to harm them. The culture of the people of Daleside is well preserved, and their community has social issues very similar to those in my own. This similarity helps me to relate with them, to some extent, but there are also differences that make it difficult for me to relate to them. For example, as an outsider, most of the time I am mistaken as someone looking for a job, or people think I am criminal—a family once asked me to sign a document before they allowed me to take any photographs. This never happened when I was with my white French collaborator—at least if it did, it was silent.

My collaboration with Cyprien was very important not only for our friendship and for producing this work but also to understand better the landscape we were working in, we both needed each other for energy sake and confidence.

DALESIDE REVISITED

SIDE

LINDOKUHLE **SOBEKWA**

ST

First published in 2020 by
GOST Books London

info@gostbooks.com
gostbooks.com

Edited and designed by GOST:
Katie Clifford, Gemma Gerhard, Allon Kaye, Eleanor Macnair, Claudia Paladini, Ana Rocha, Justine Schuster

Printed in Italy by EBS

British Library cataloguing-in-publication data. A catalogue record of this book is available from the British Library.

isbn 978-1-910401-52-1

CYPRIEN **CLÉMENT-DELMAS**

DALE

GO

Daleside: Static Dreams is the result of a commission by Rubis Mécénat to French and South African photographers Cyprien Clément-Delmas and Lindokuhle Sobekwa, within the frame of its Of Soul and Joy project, a platform for learning photography in the township of Thokoza in South Africa. The book is a culmination of the five-year photographic project dedicated to Daleside, a small Afrikaner town located in South Africa's Gauteng province.

For the commission, Cyprien Clément-Delmas and Lindokuhle Sobekwa were able to revisit together the validity of this white enclave, which, although it is bordered by the highway that connects it to Johannesburg, remains isolated in its large industrial periphery. At a distance, Daleside keeps its white population in seclusion, forgotten in an old project of 'separate development.'
The photographers drew a portrait of Daleside, approached the place and the inhabitants, mostly miners or small farmers, awakening their dreams or revealing their distress.

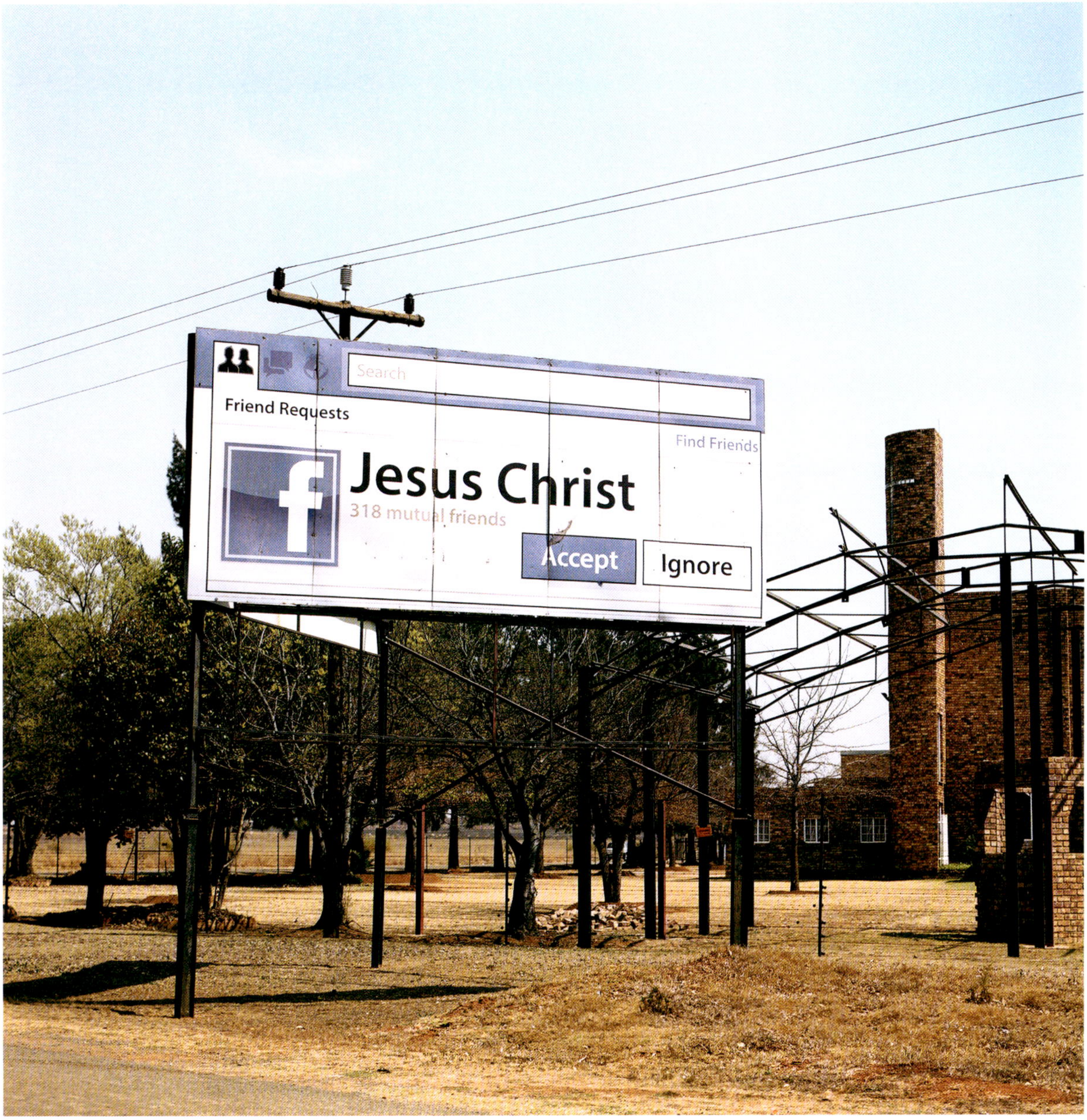
Search
Friend Requests
Find Friends
Jesus Christ
318 mutual friends
Accept
Ignore

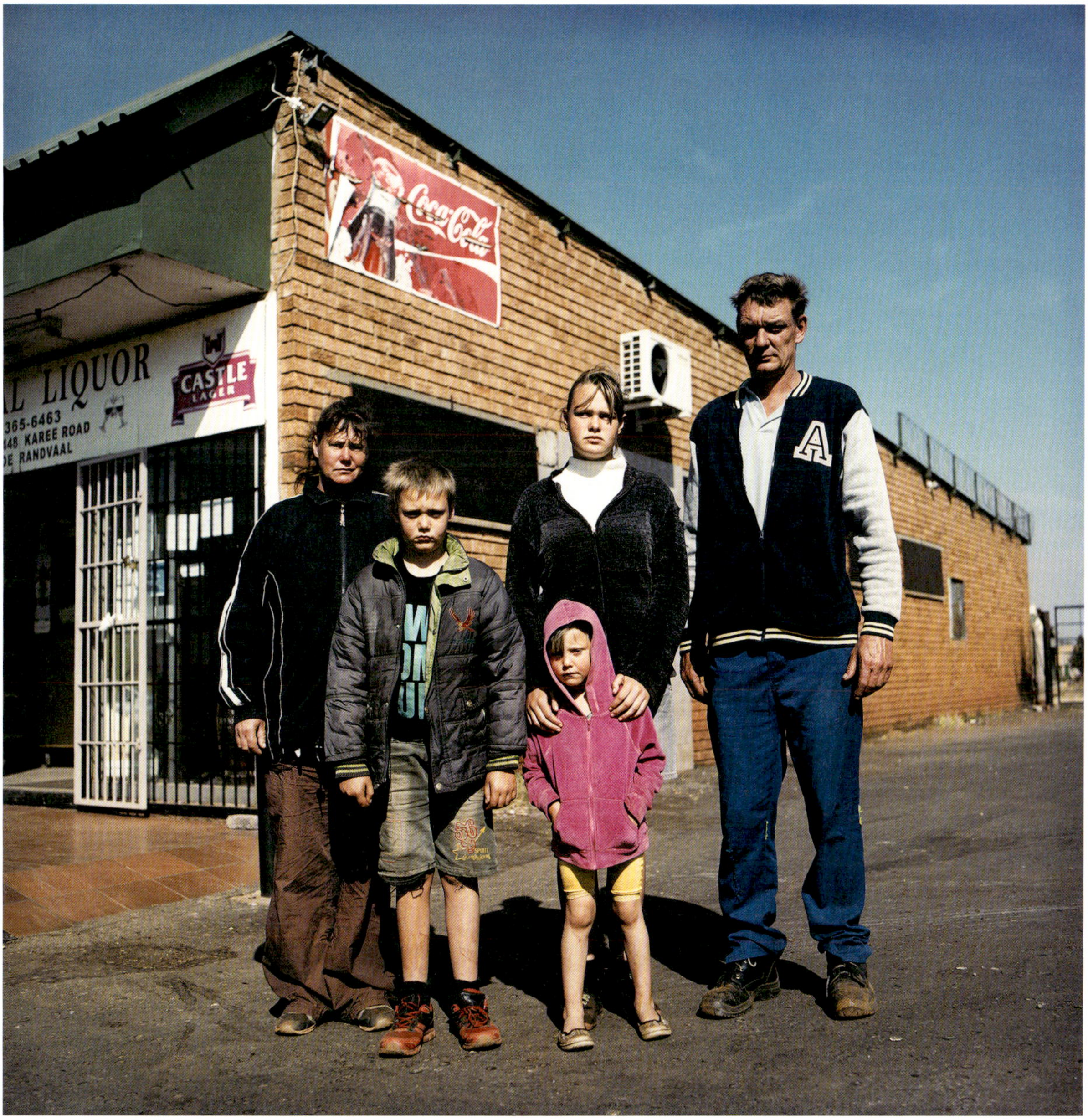
Coca-Cola
AL LIQUOR
365-6463
348 KAREE ROAD
DE RANDVAAL
CASTLE
LAGER
A

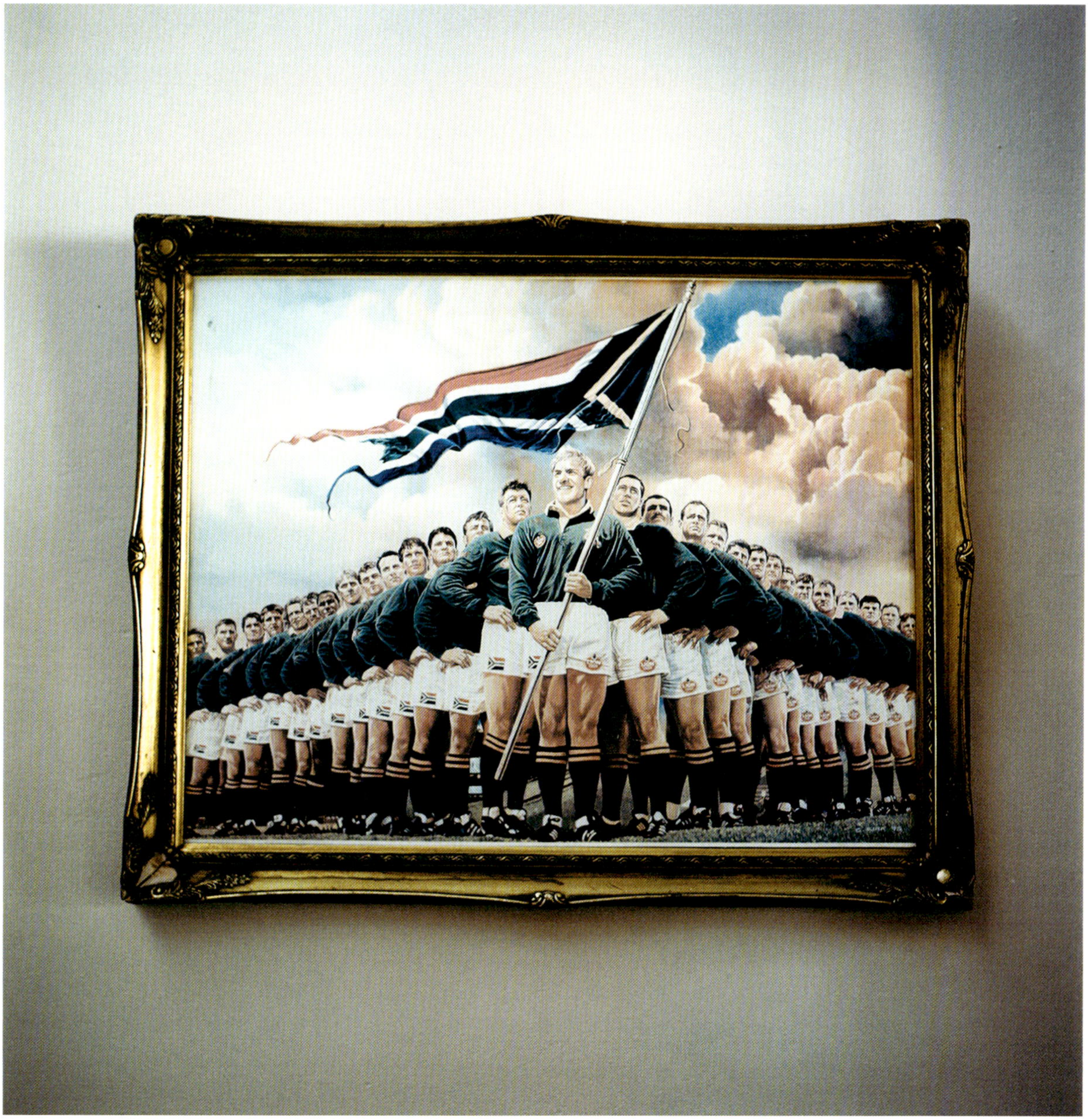

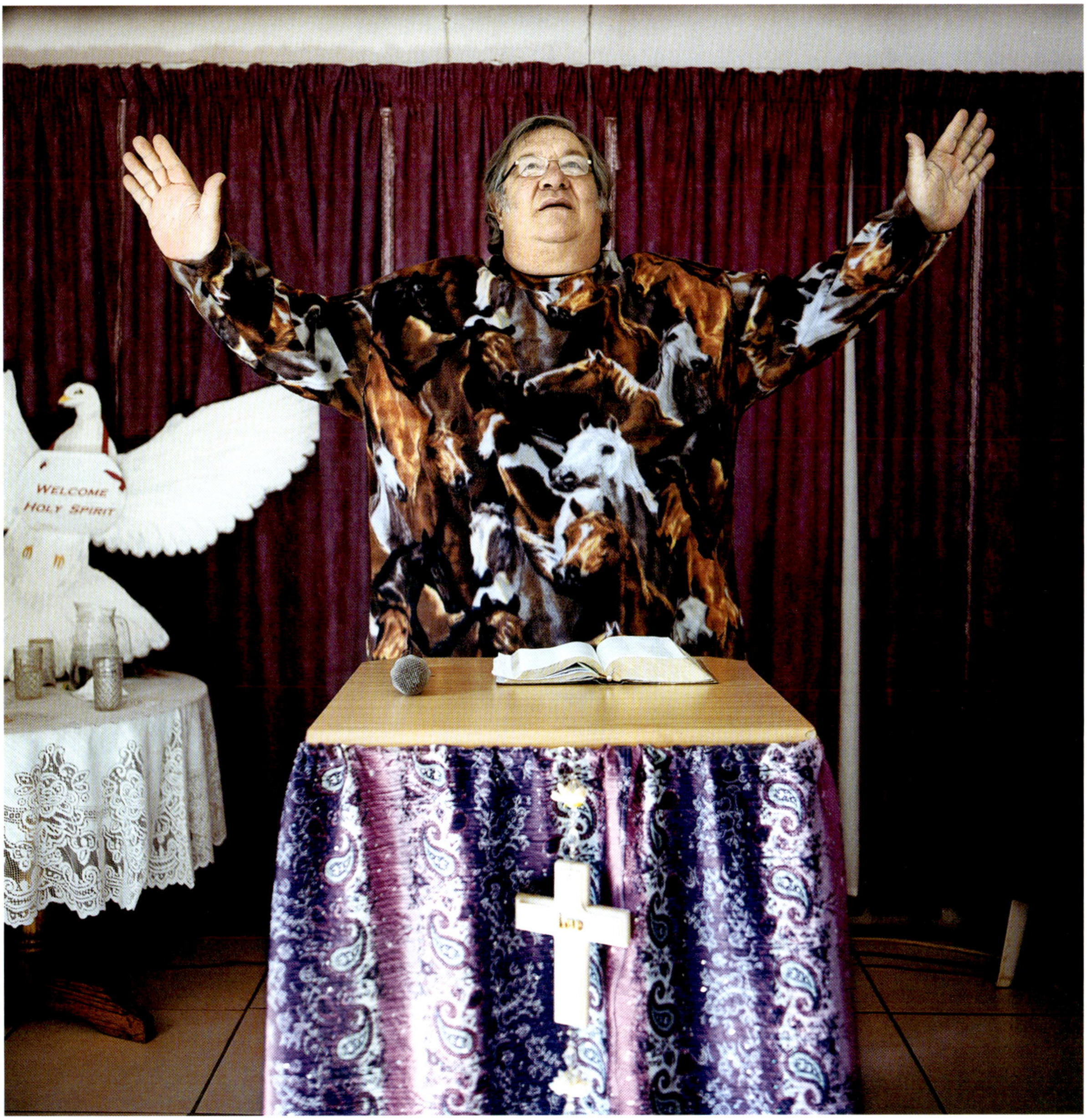
WELCOME
HOLY SPIRIT

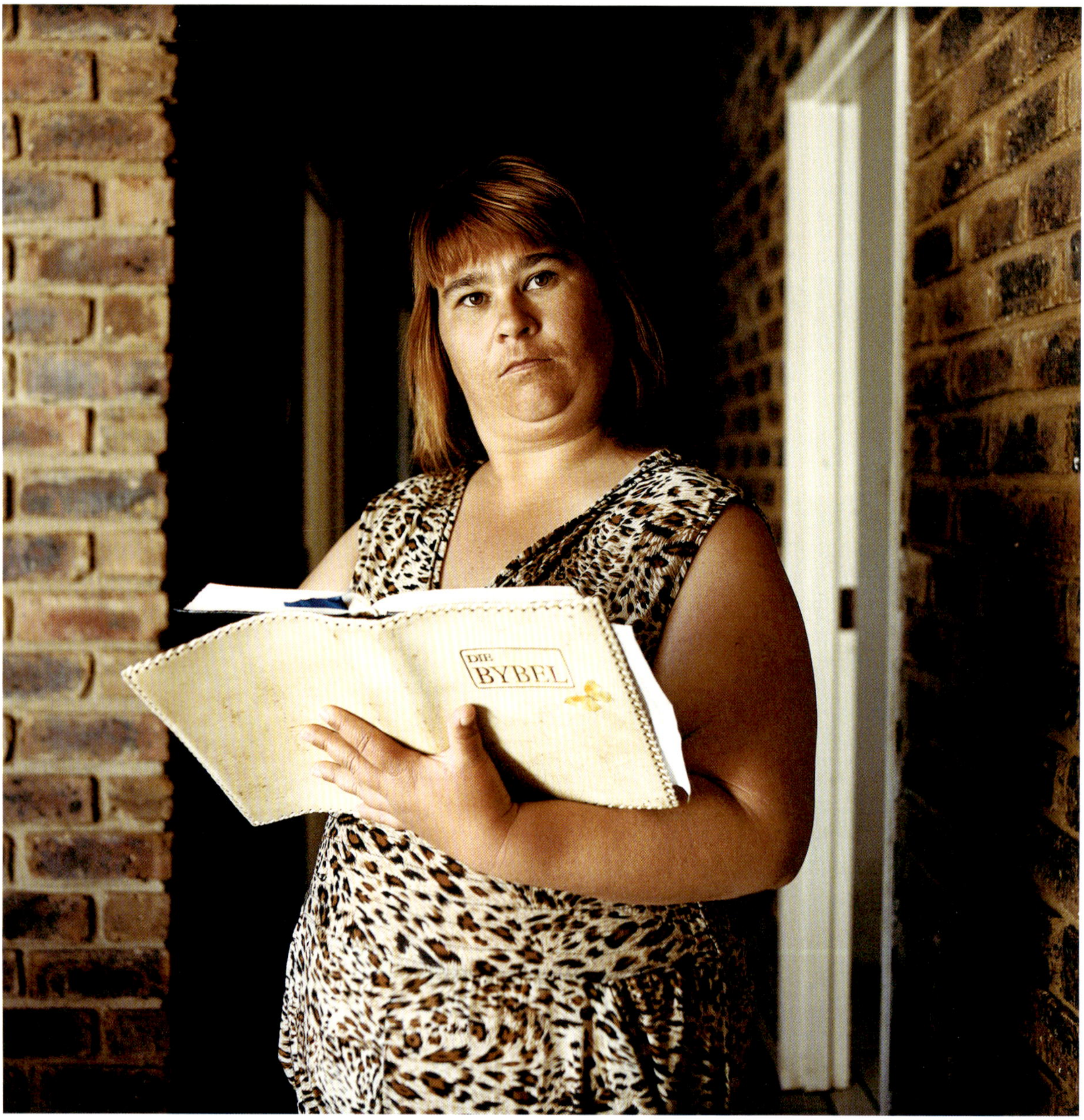
DIE
BYBEL

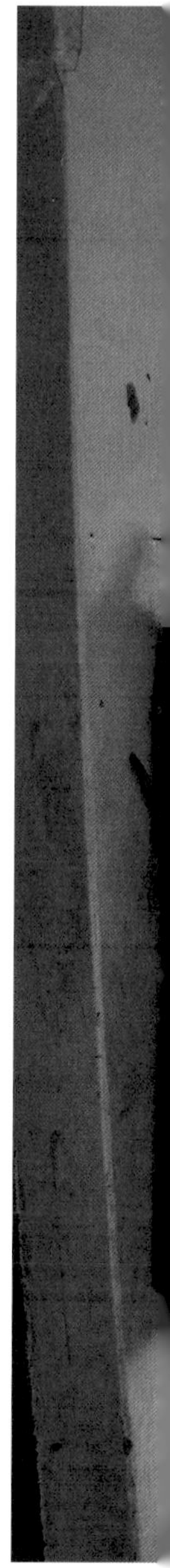

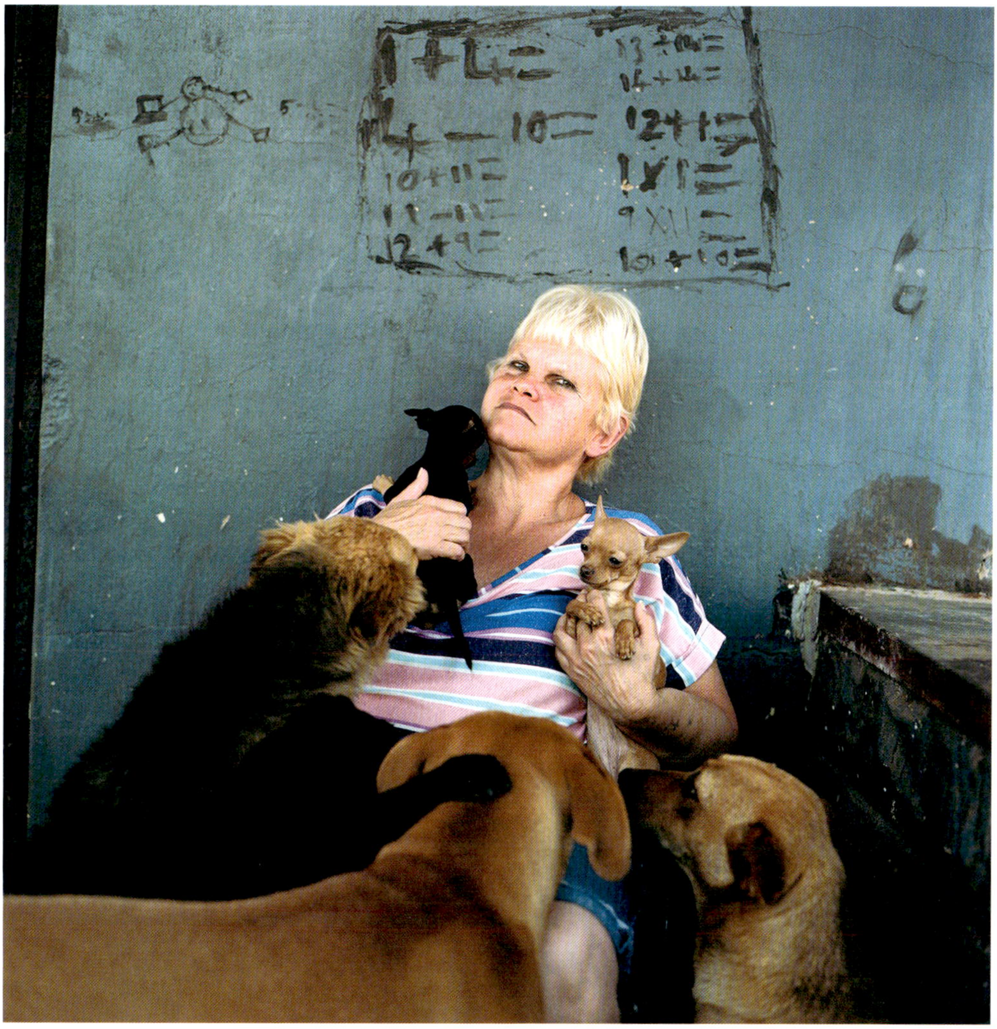

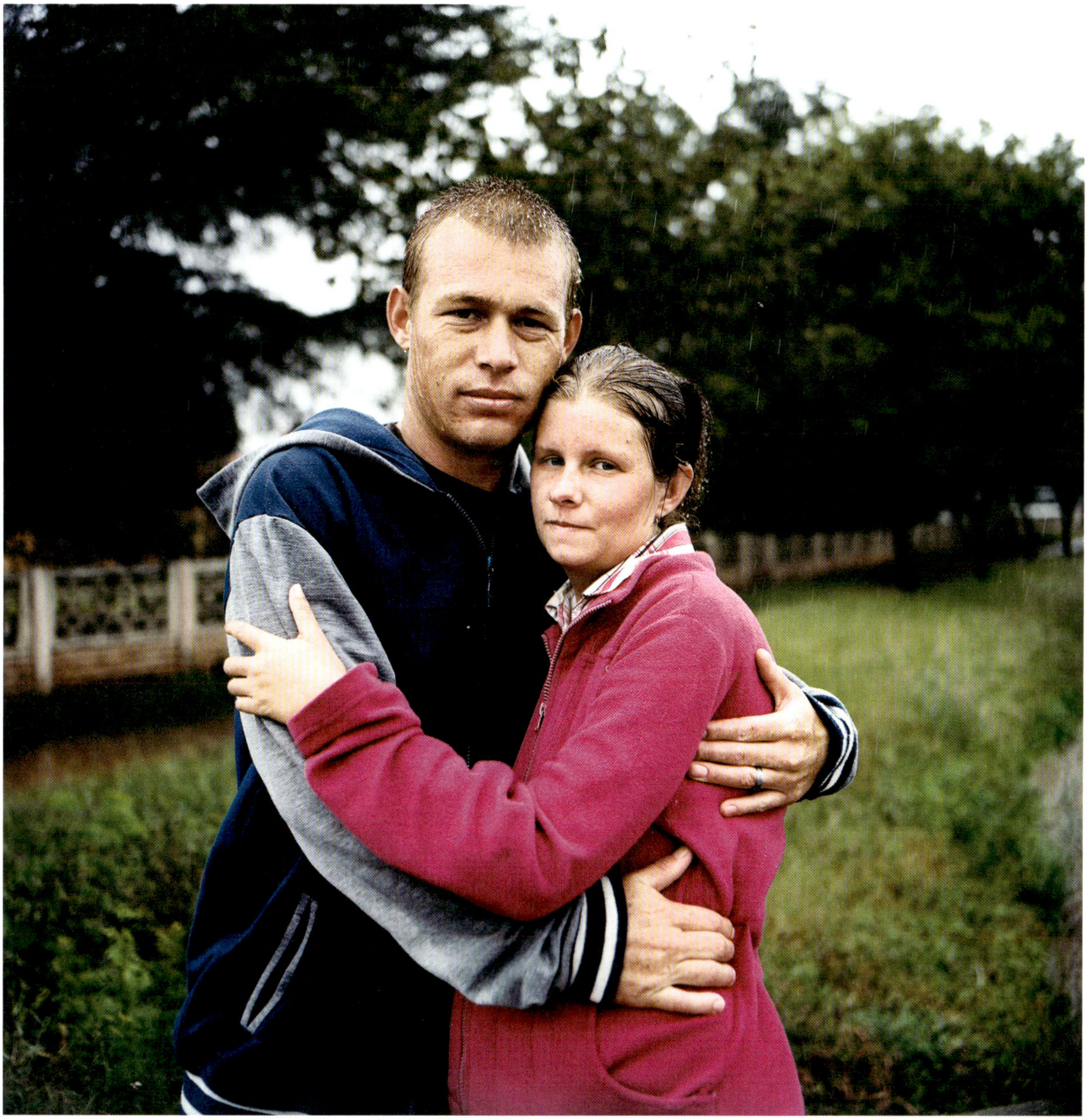

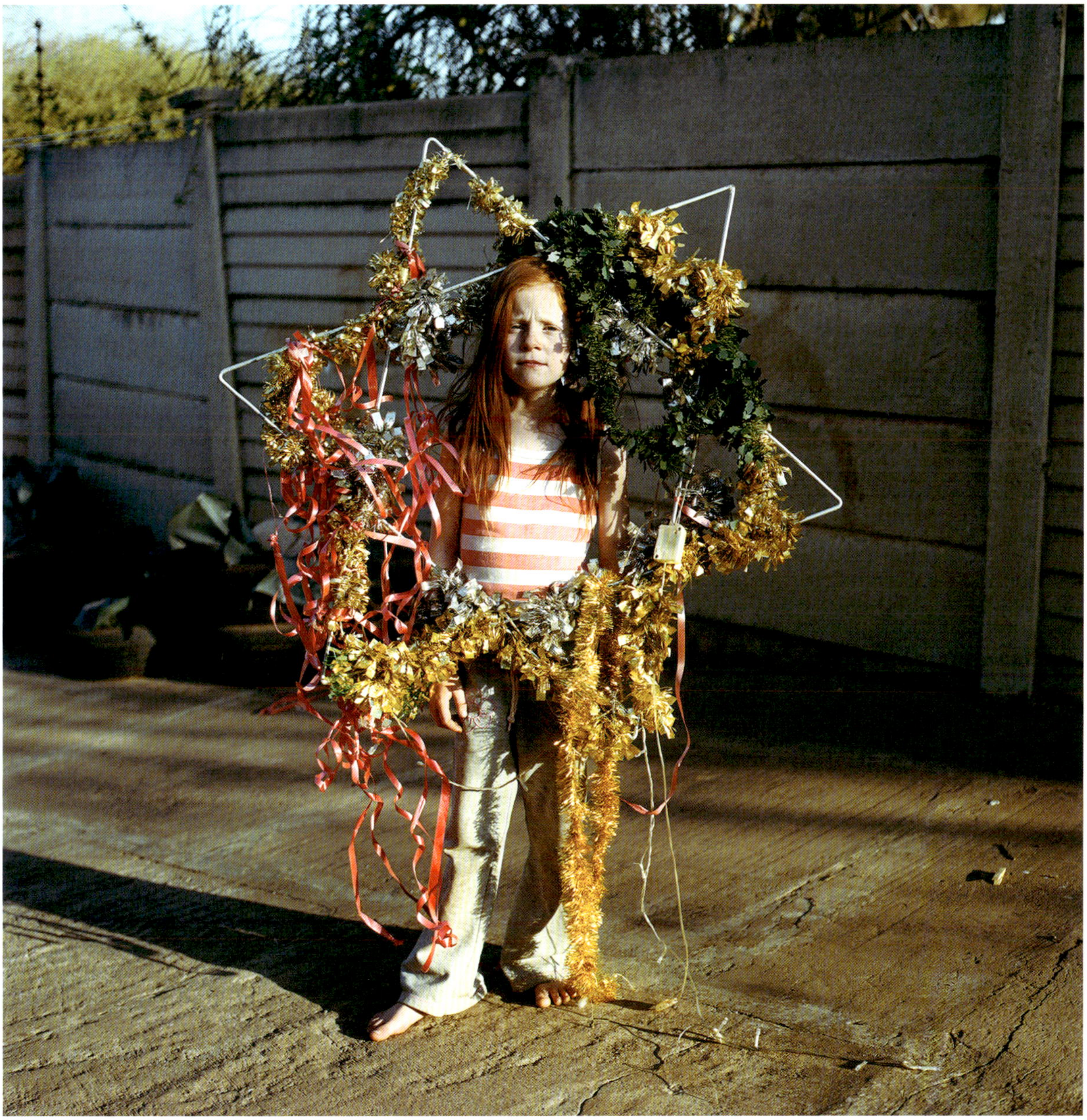

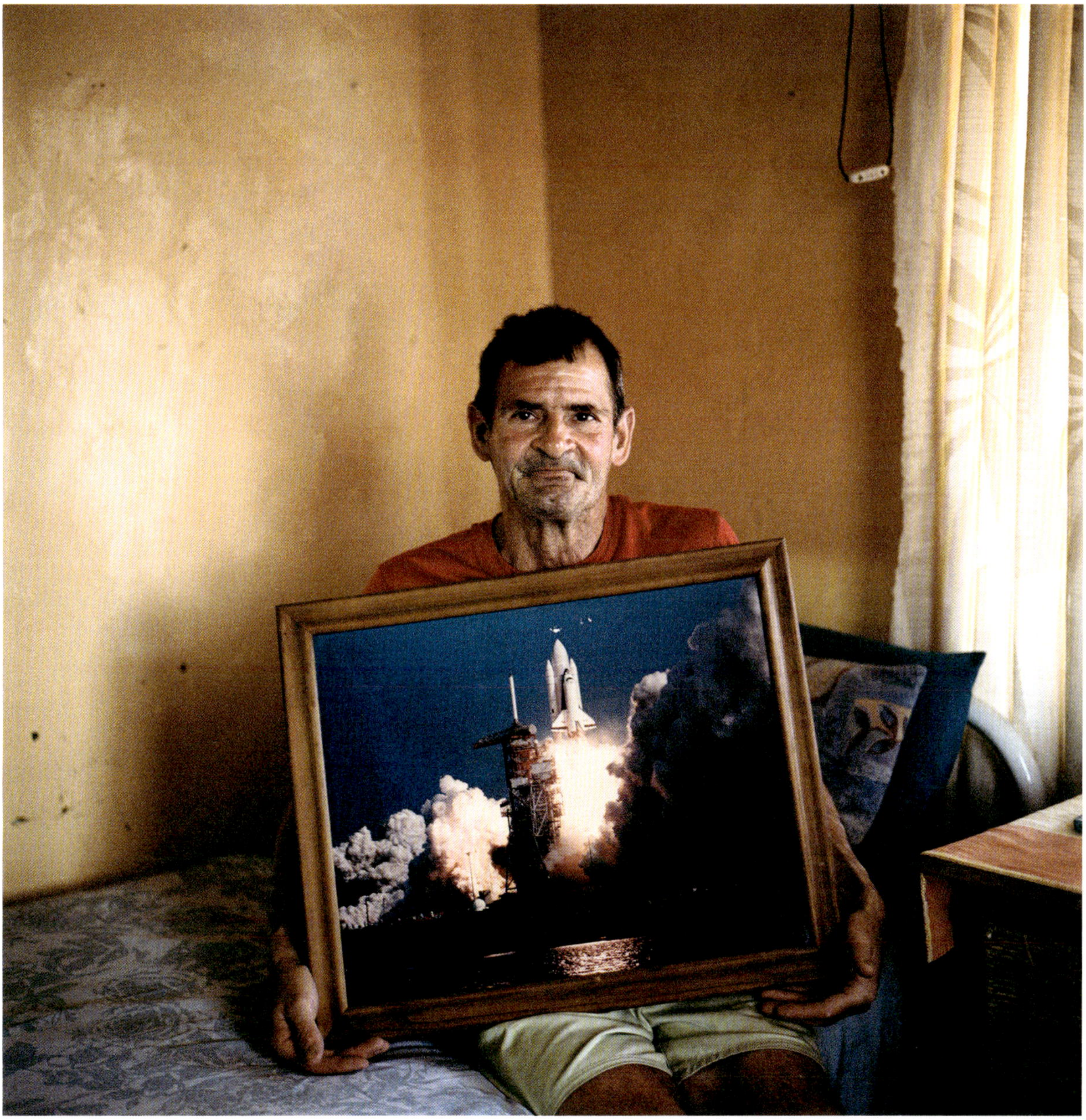

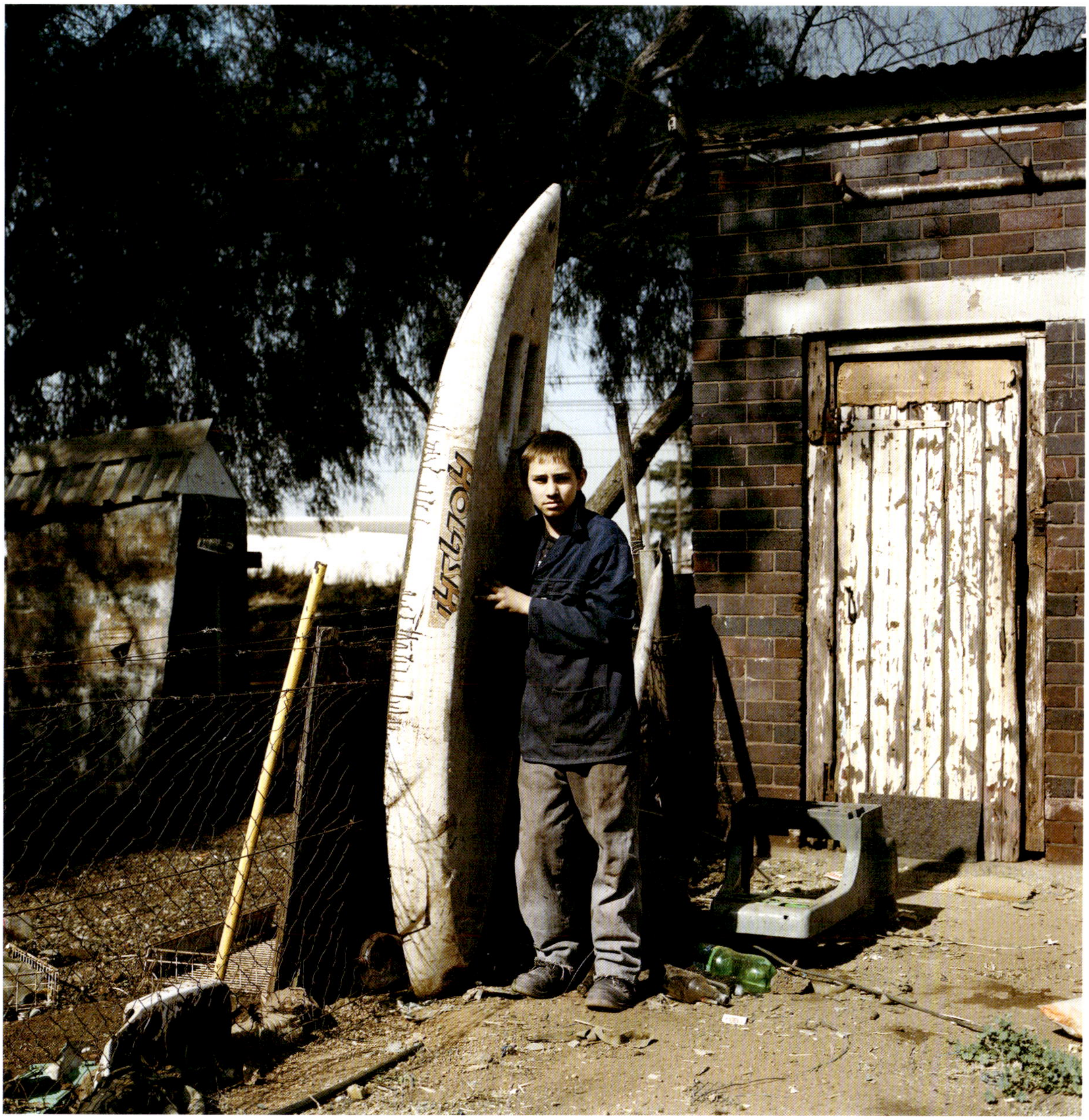

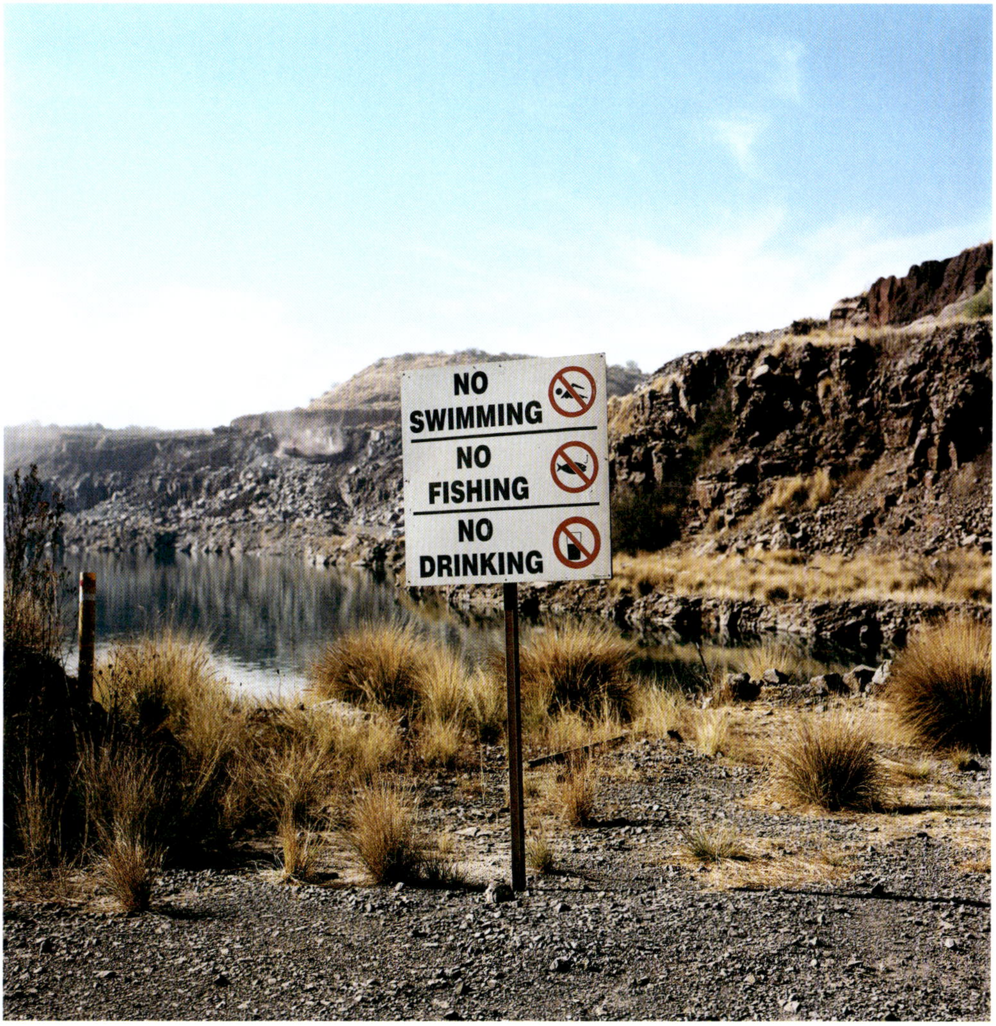
NO
SWIMMING
NO
FISHING
NO
DRINKING

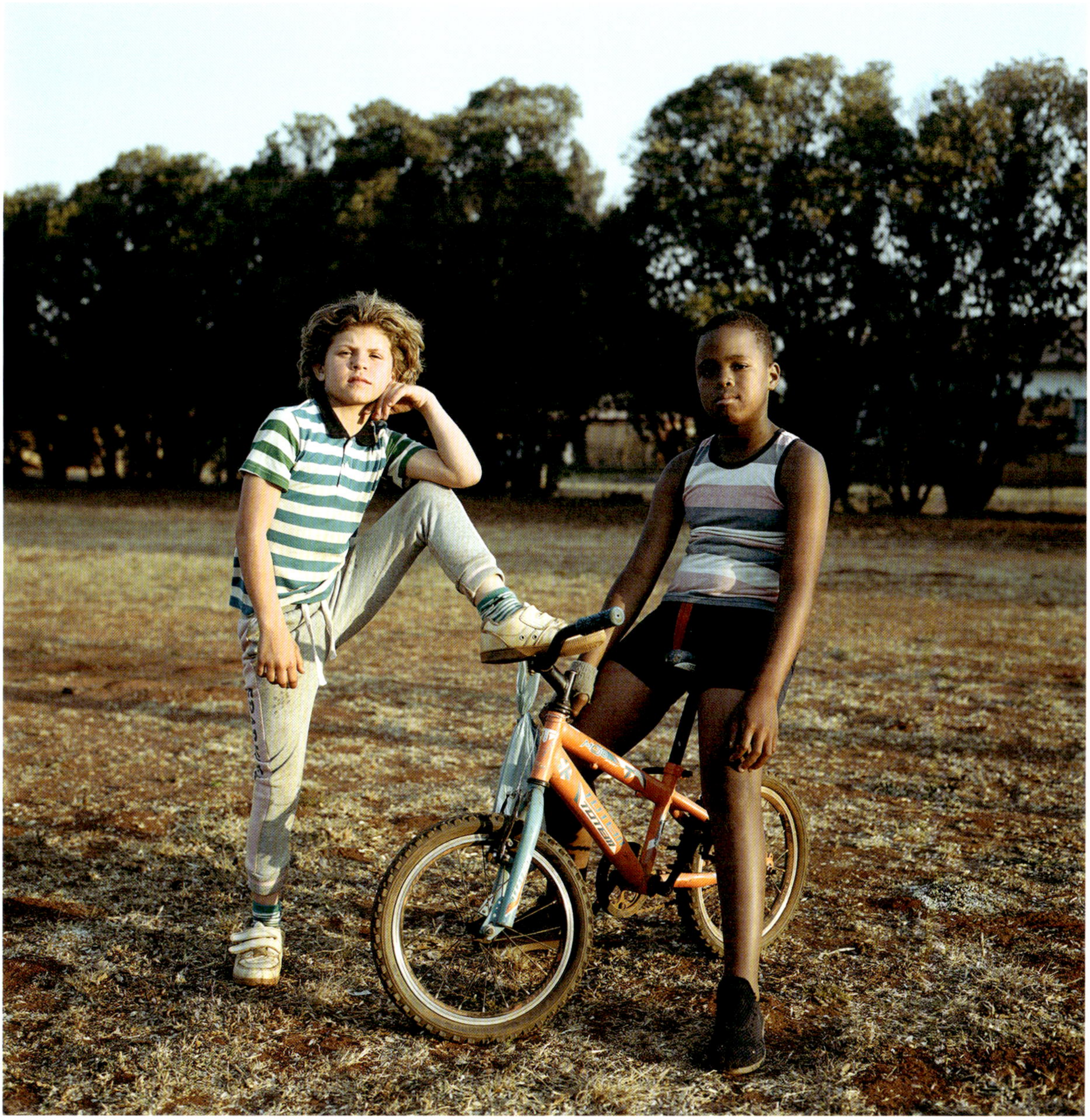

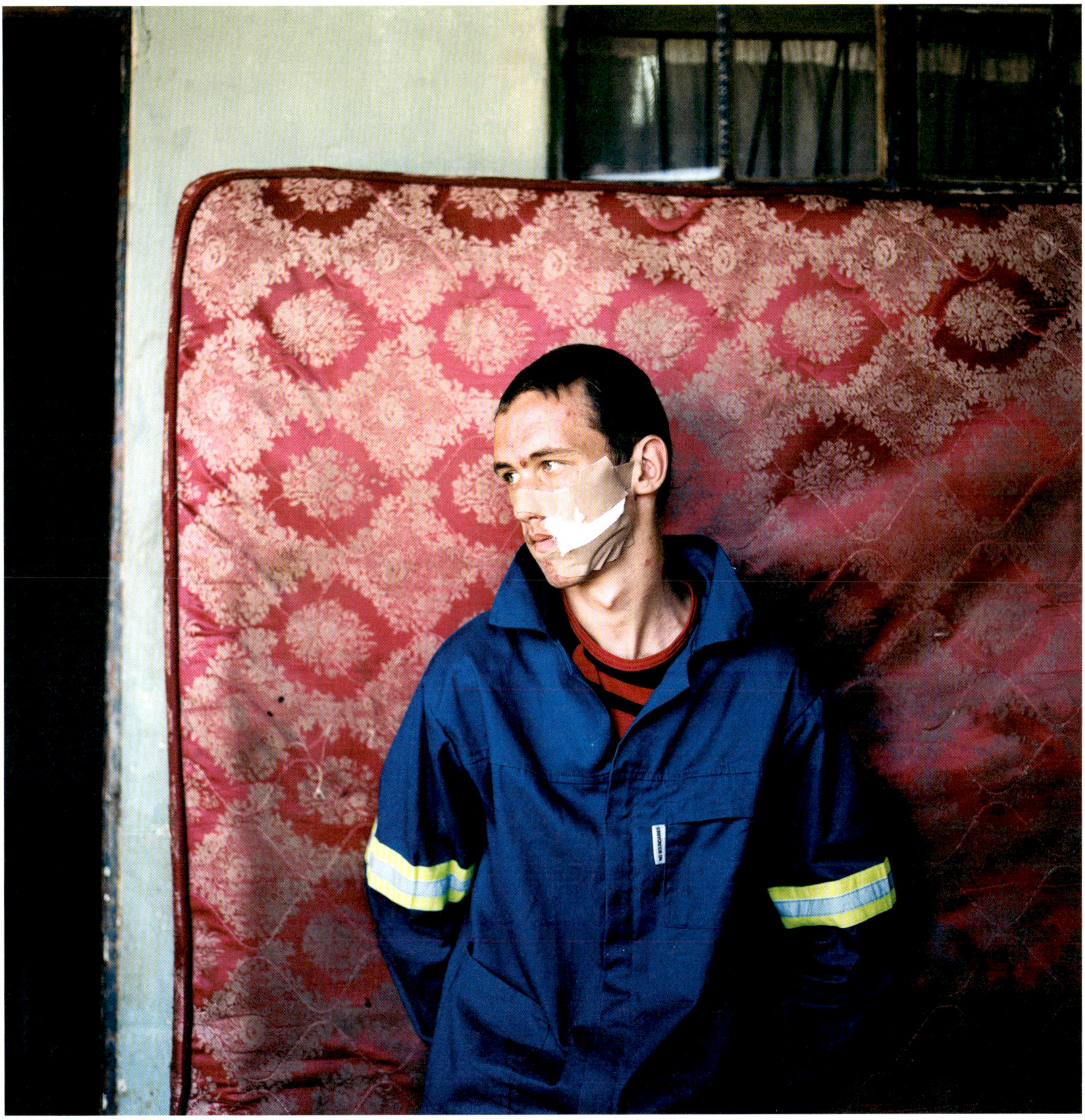

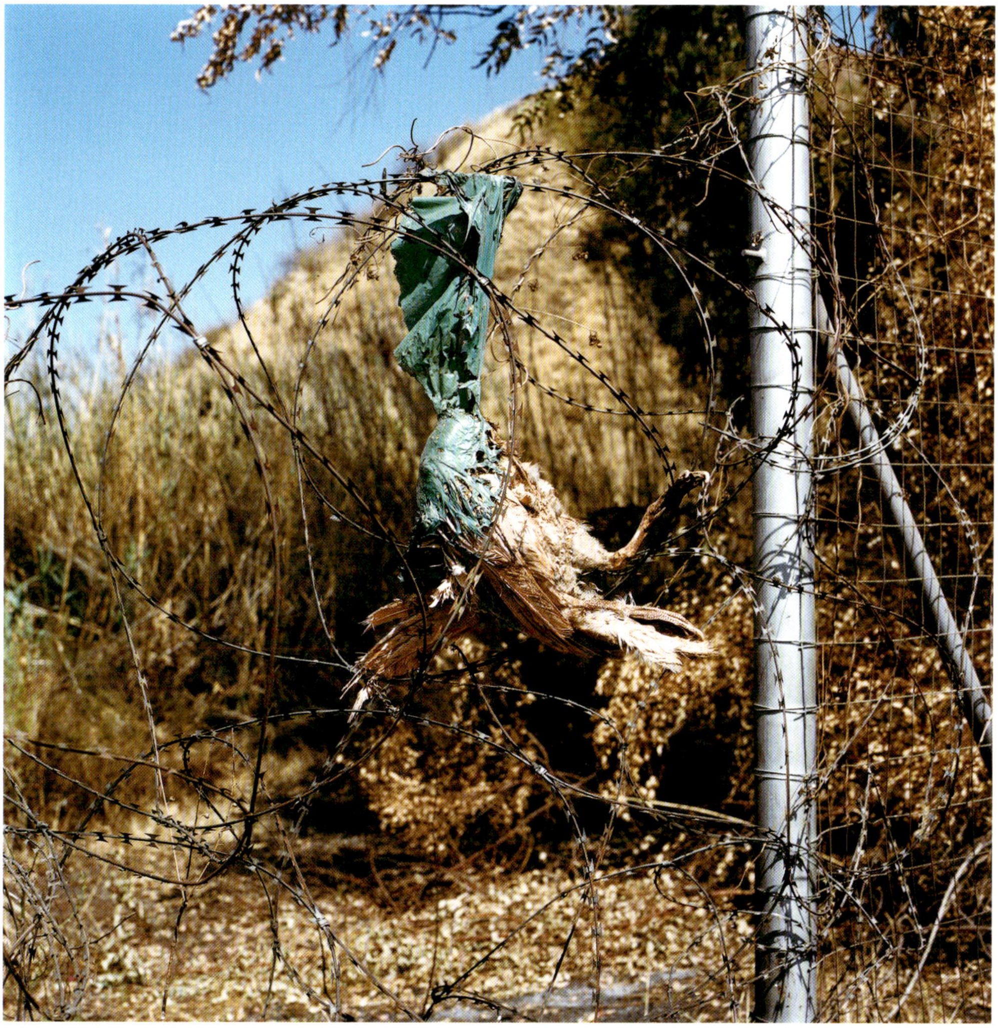

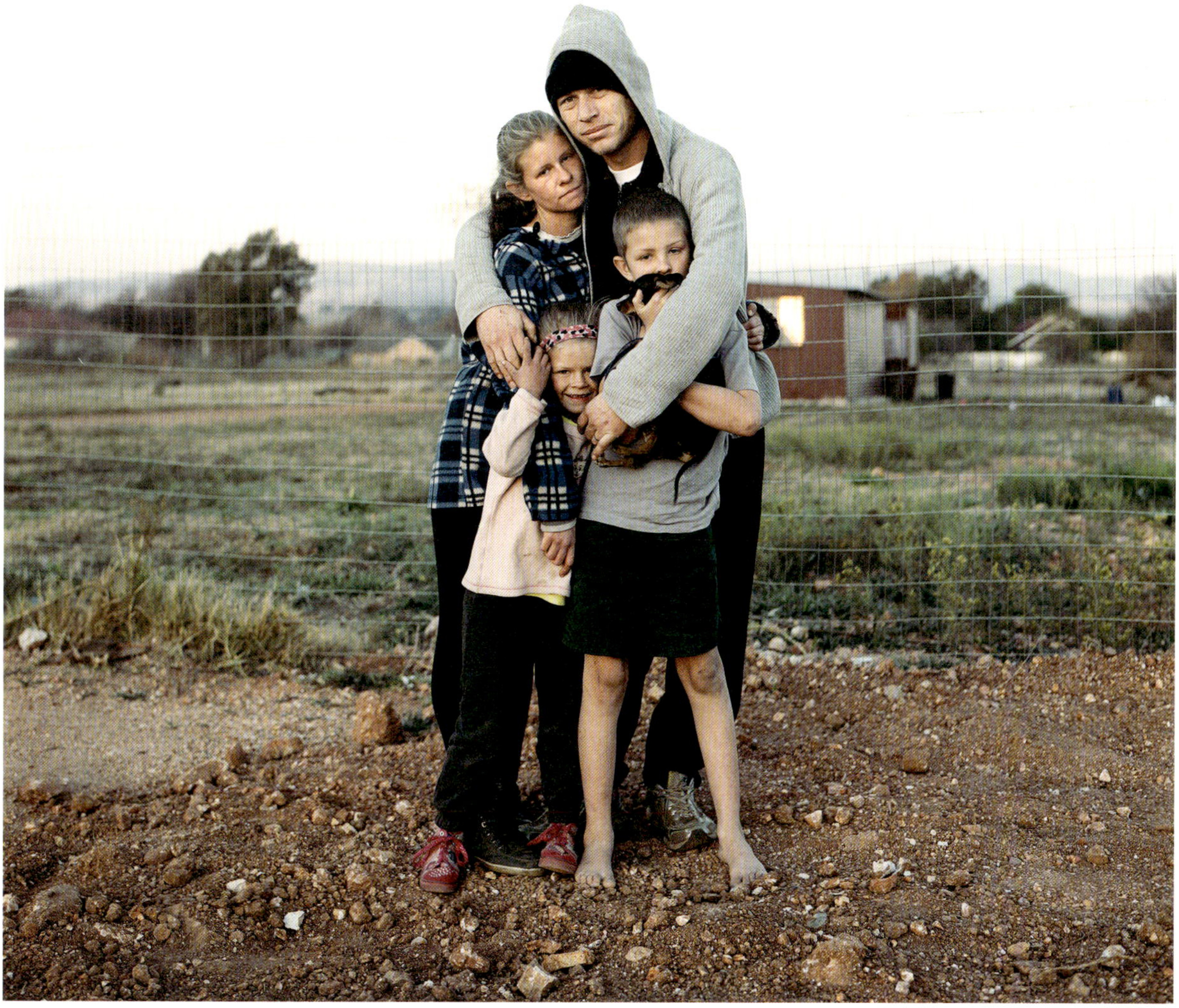

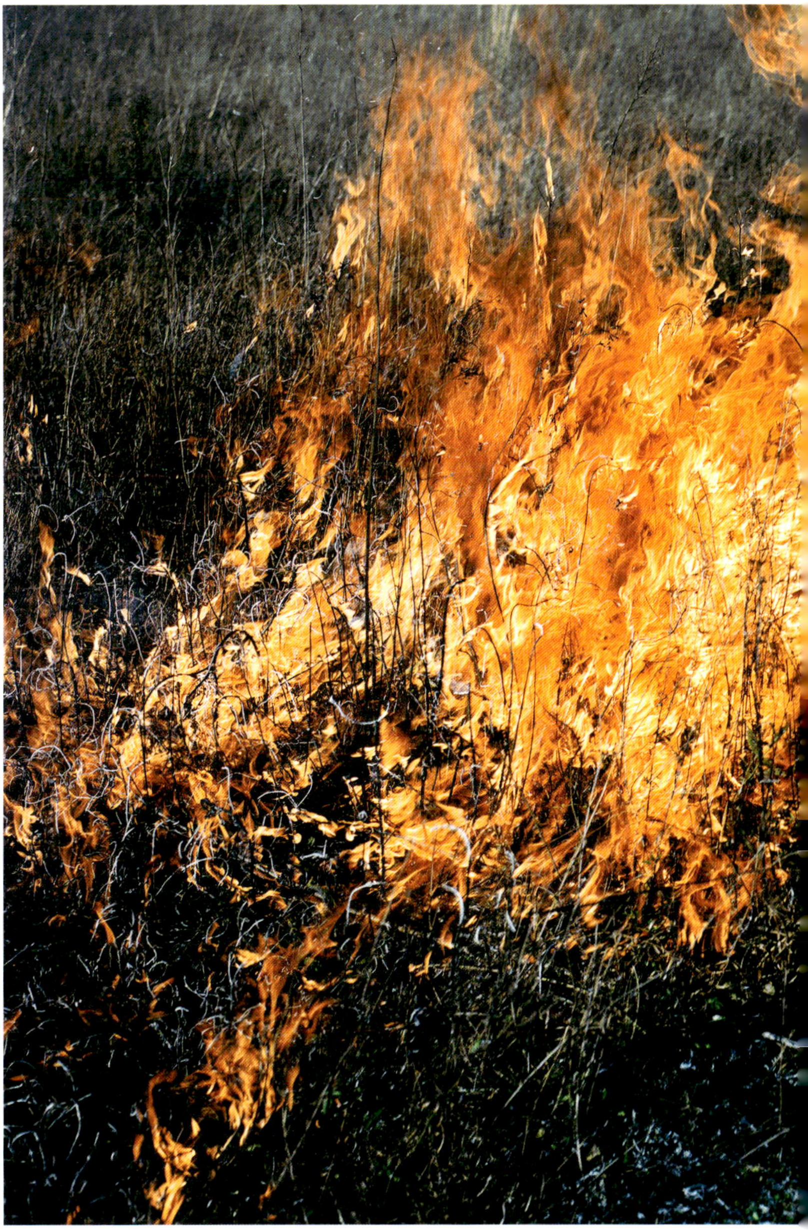

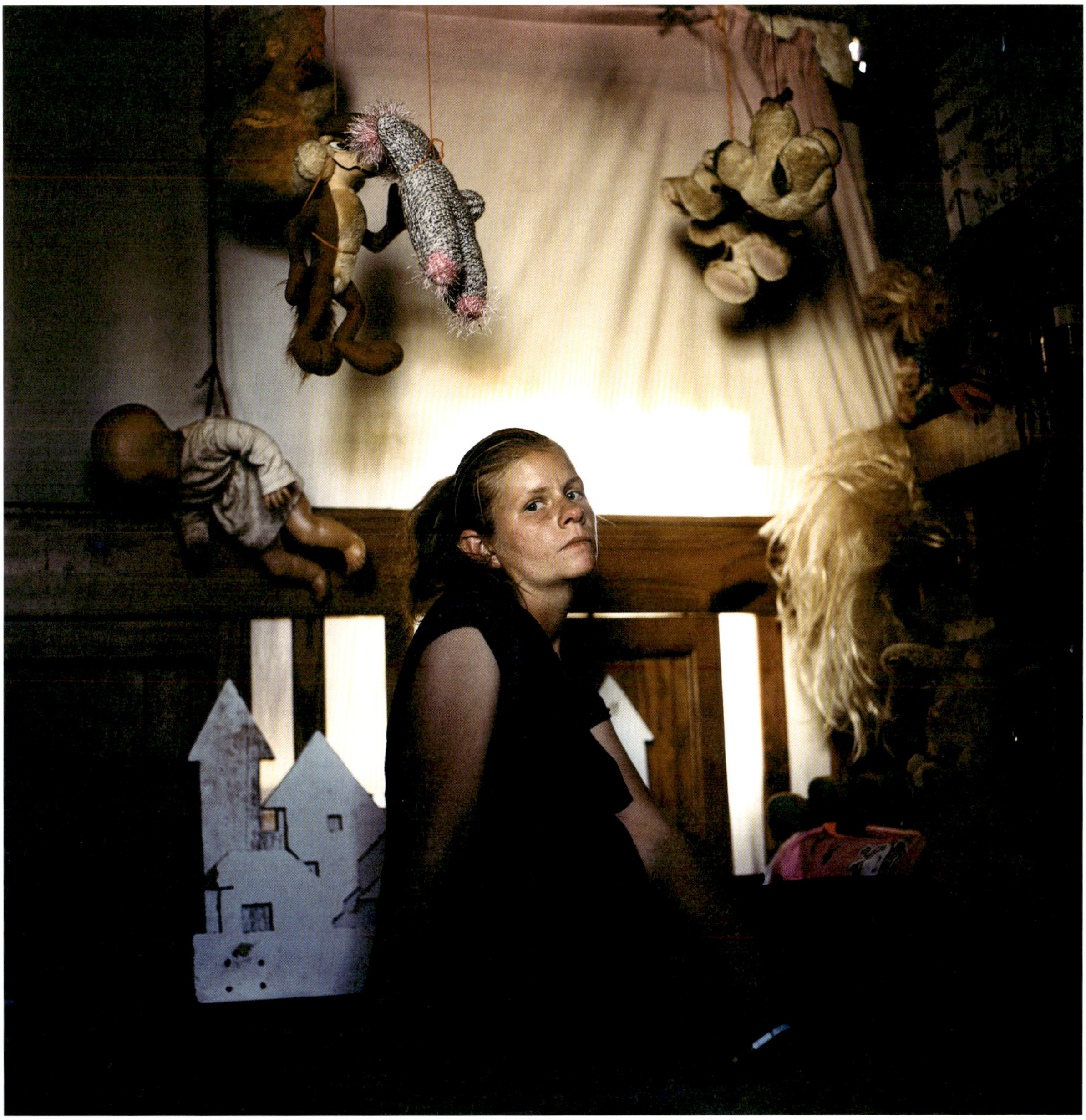

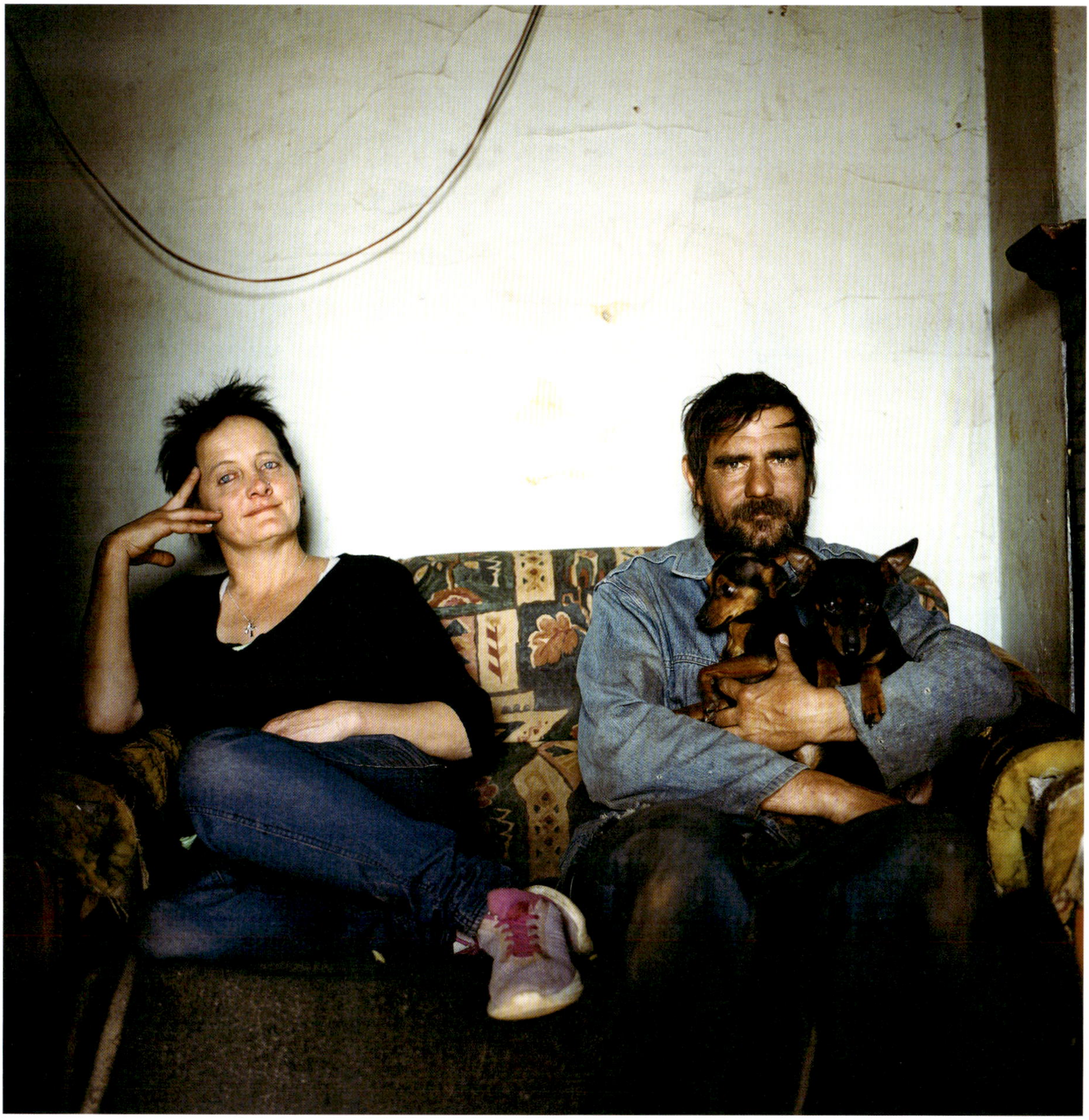

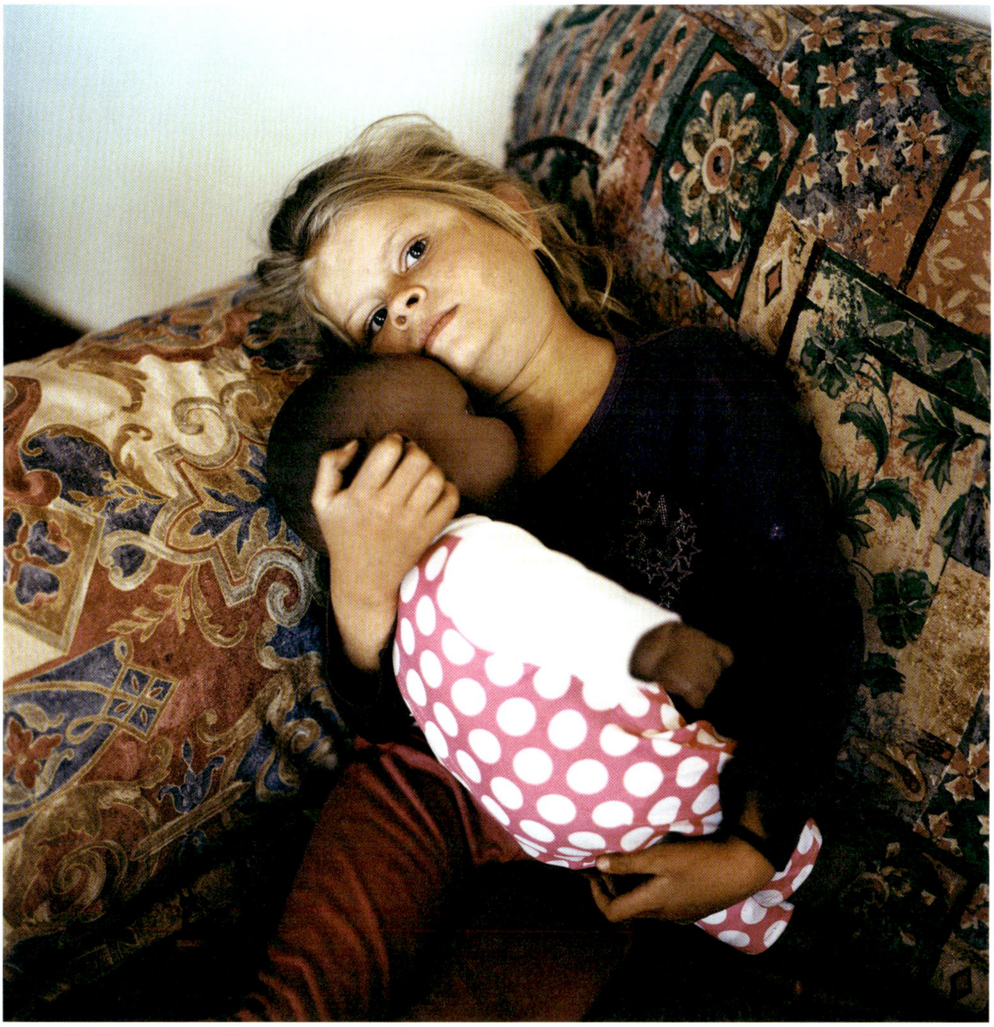

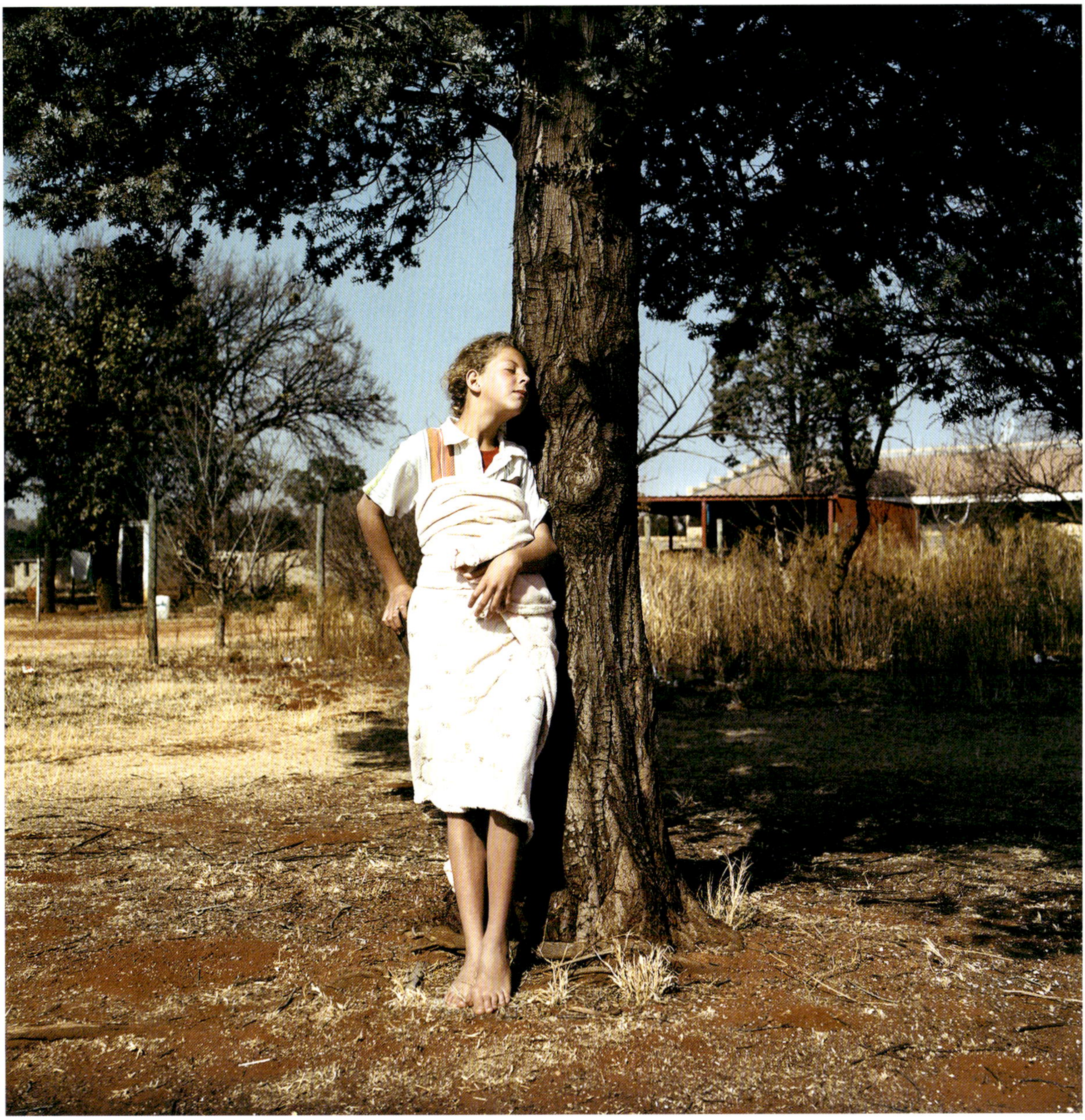

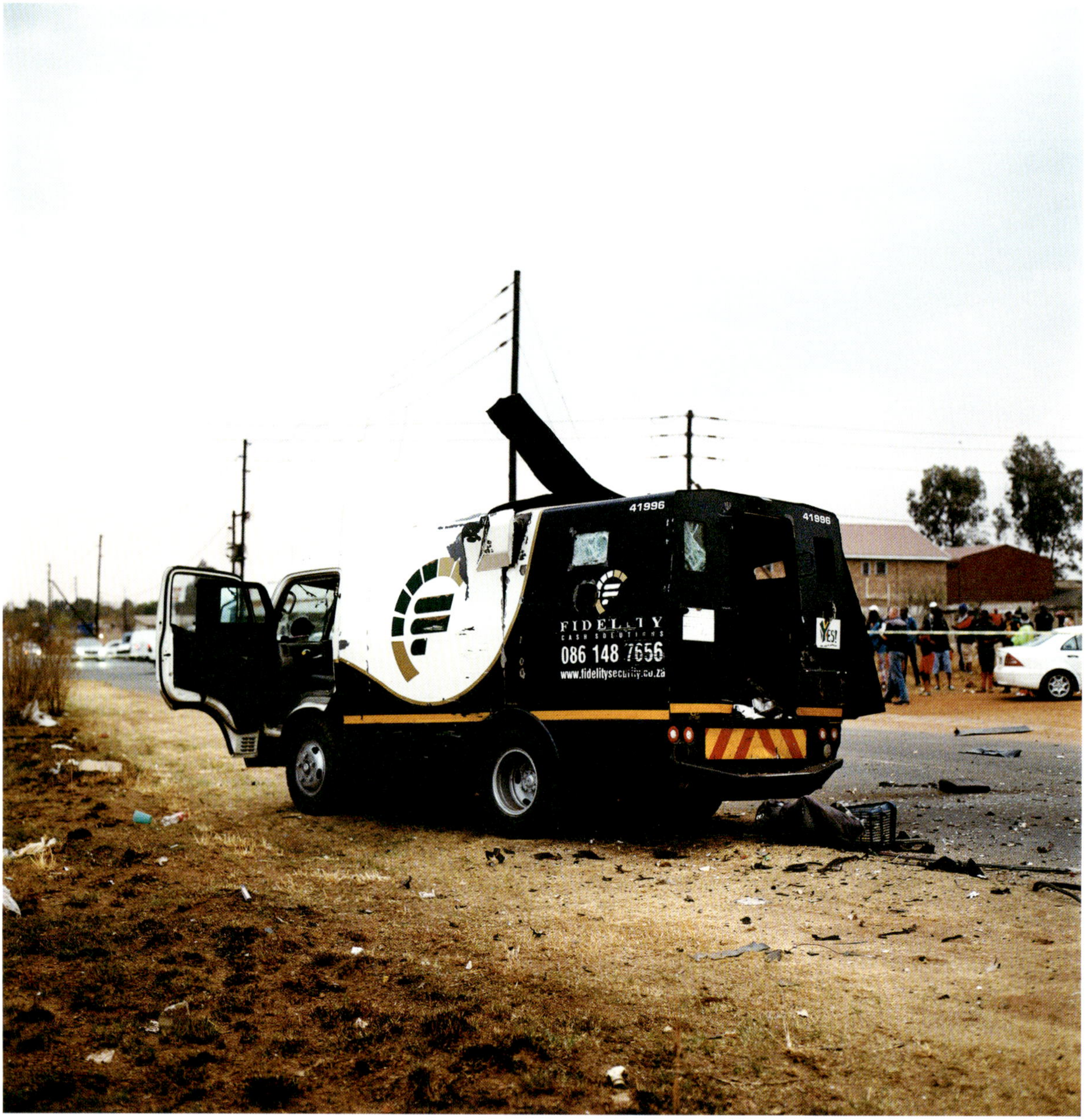

41996
41996
FIDELITY
CASH SOLUTIONS
086 148 7656
www.fidelitysecurity.co.za

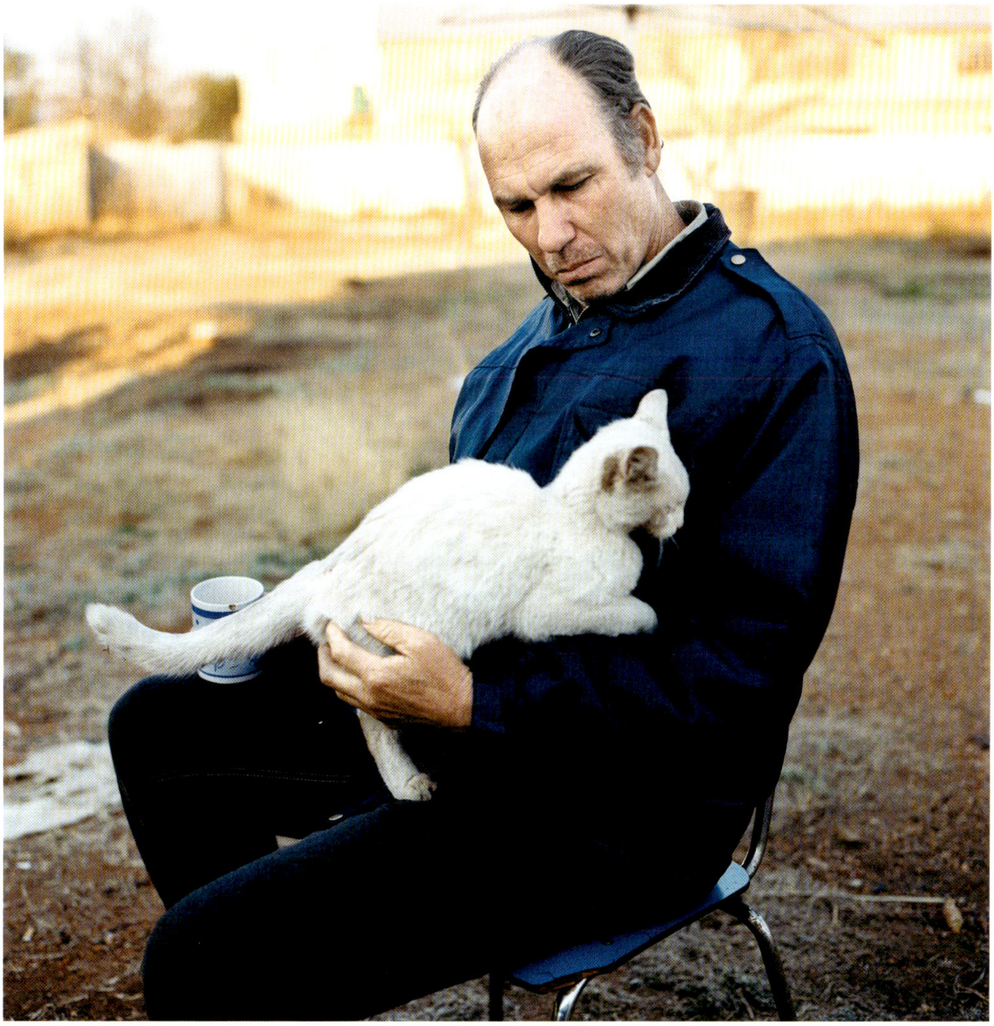

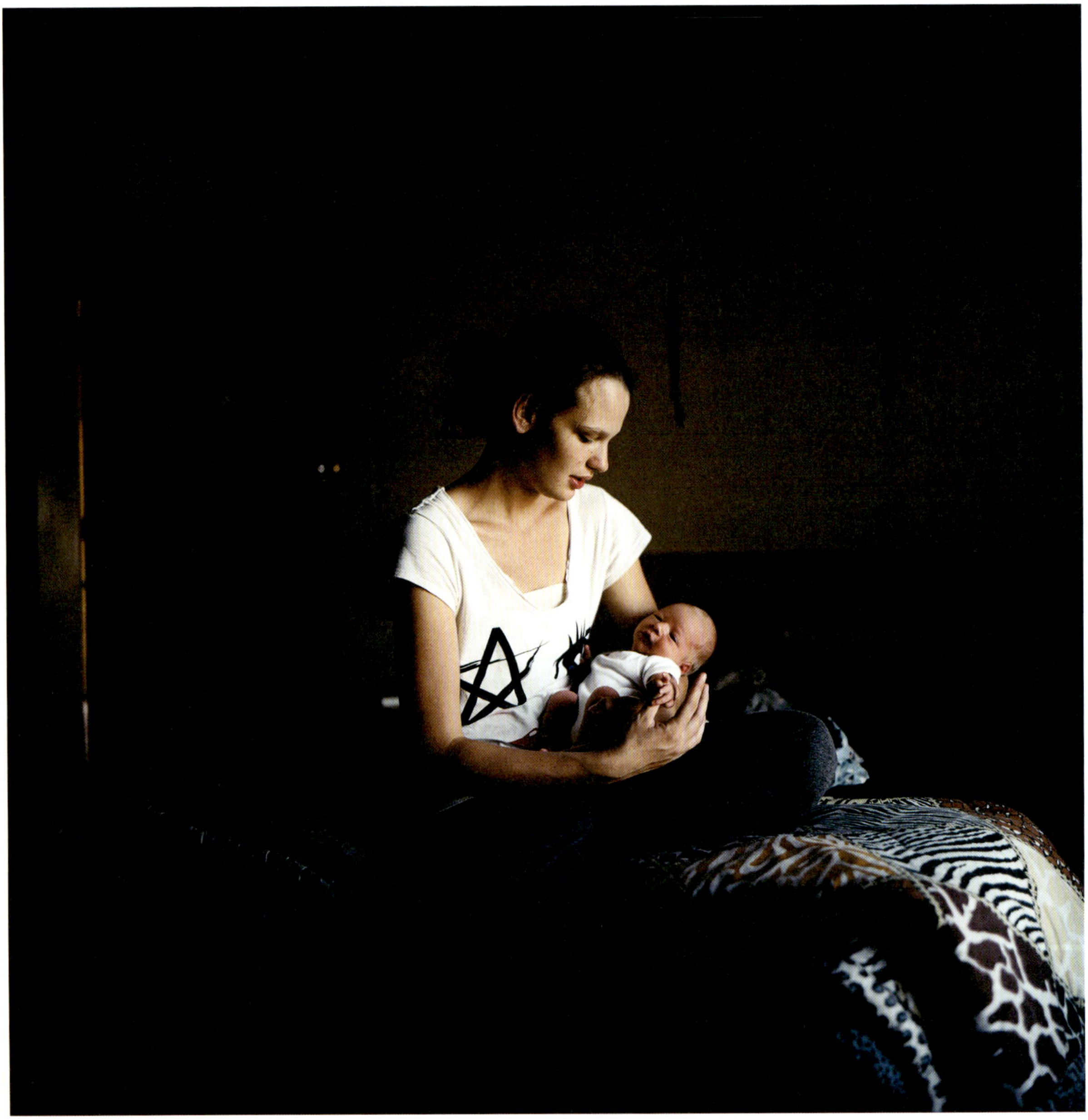

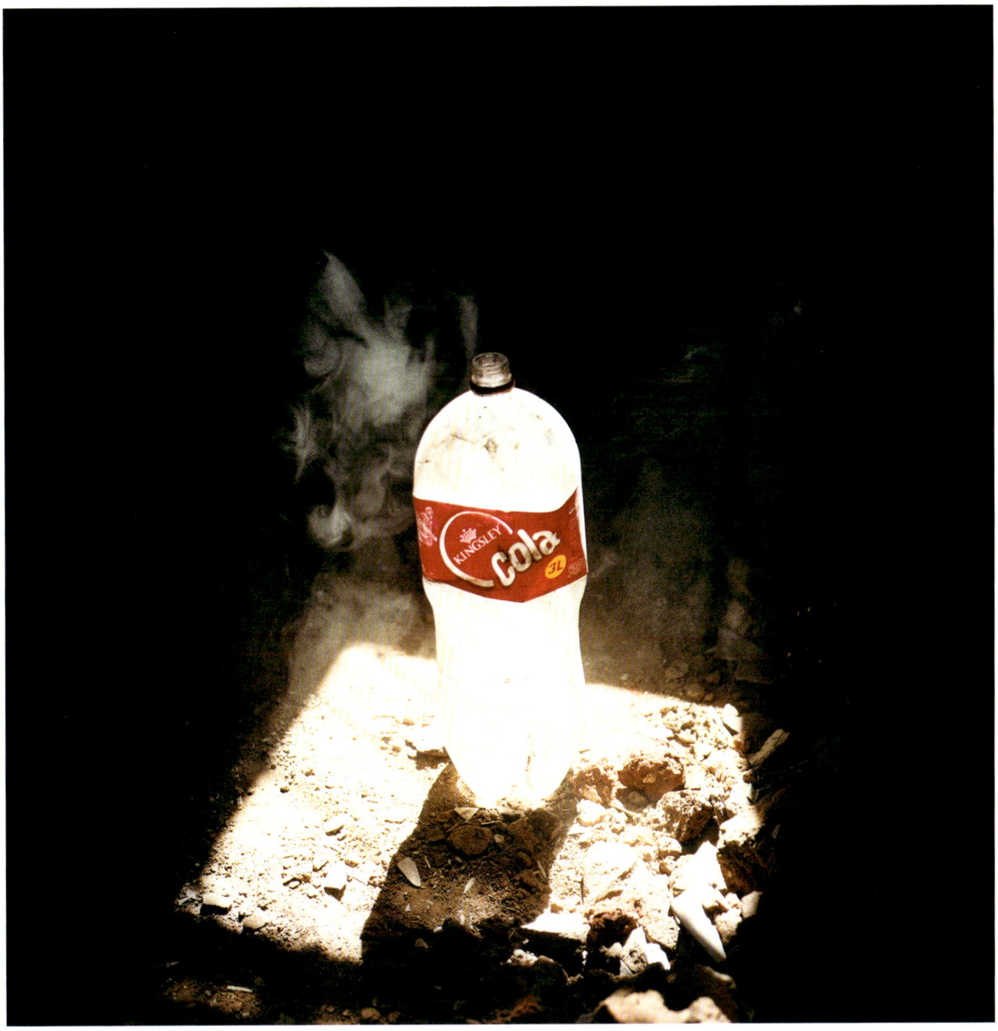
KINGSLEY
Cola

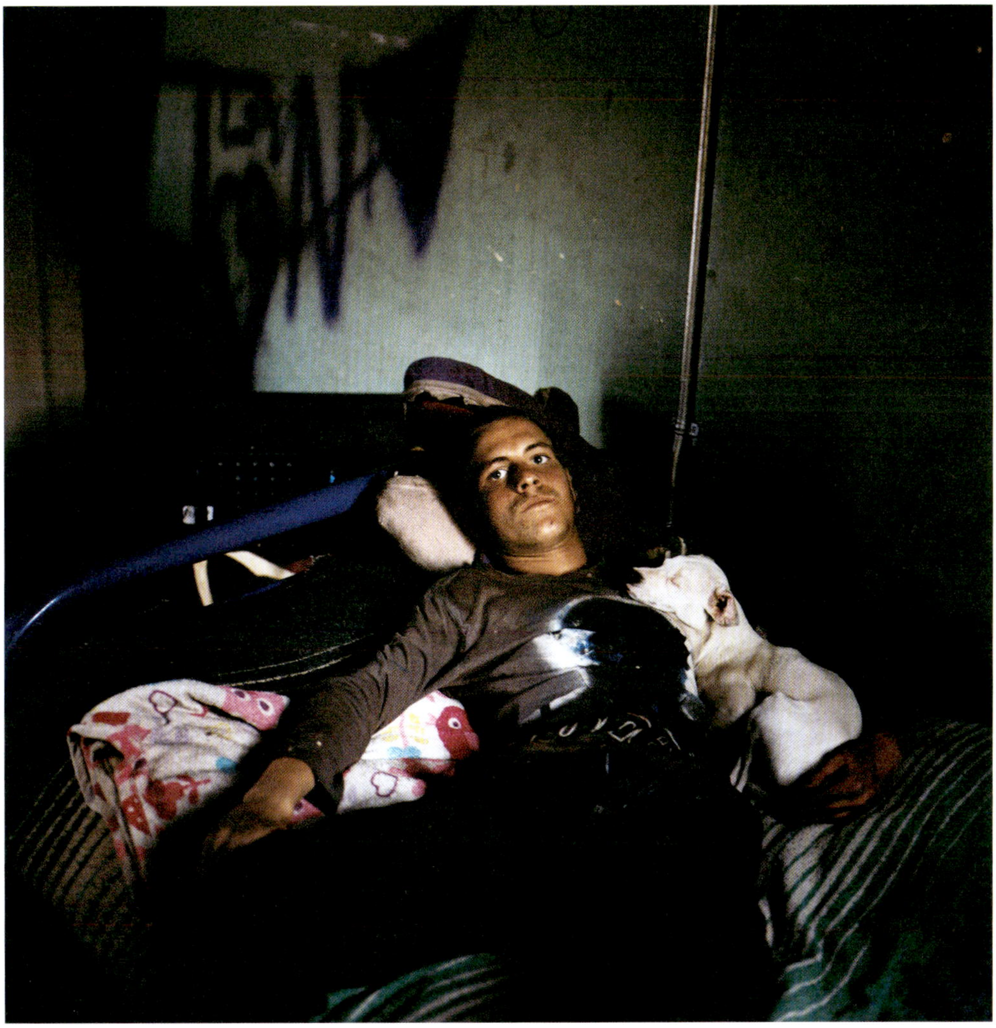

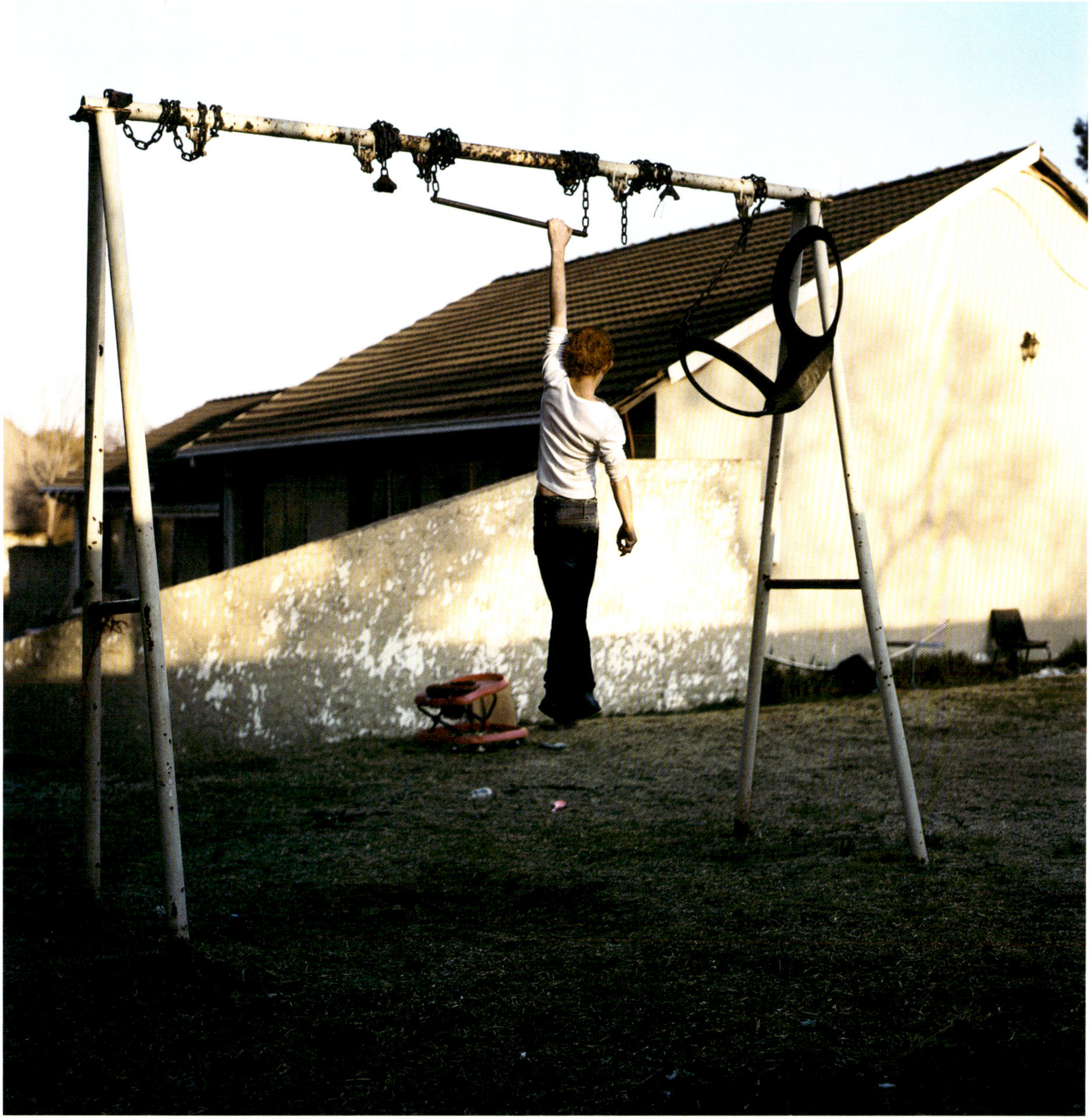

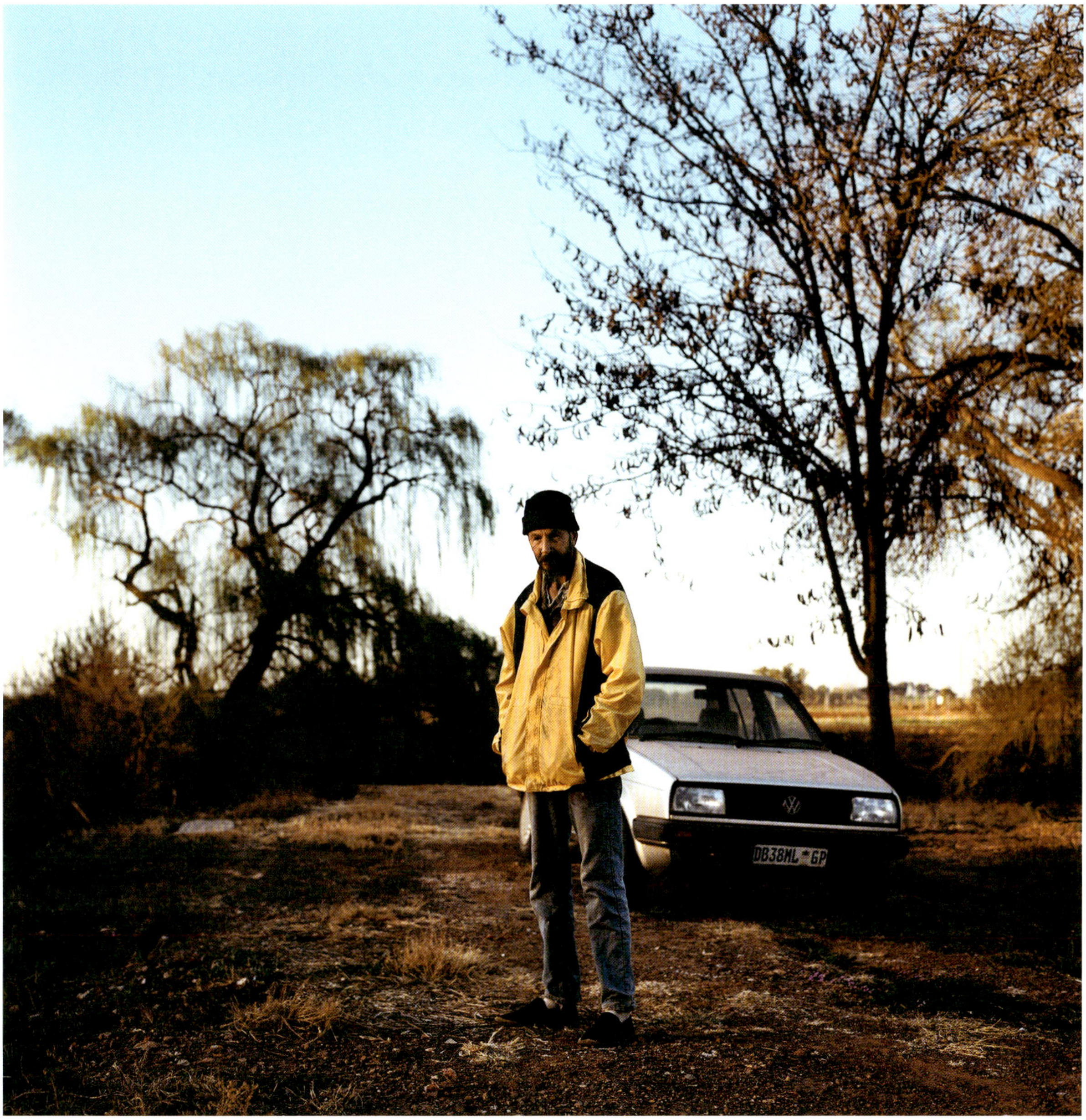
DB38ML GP

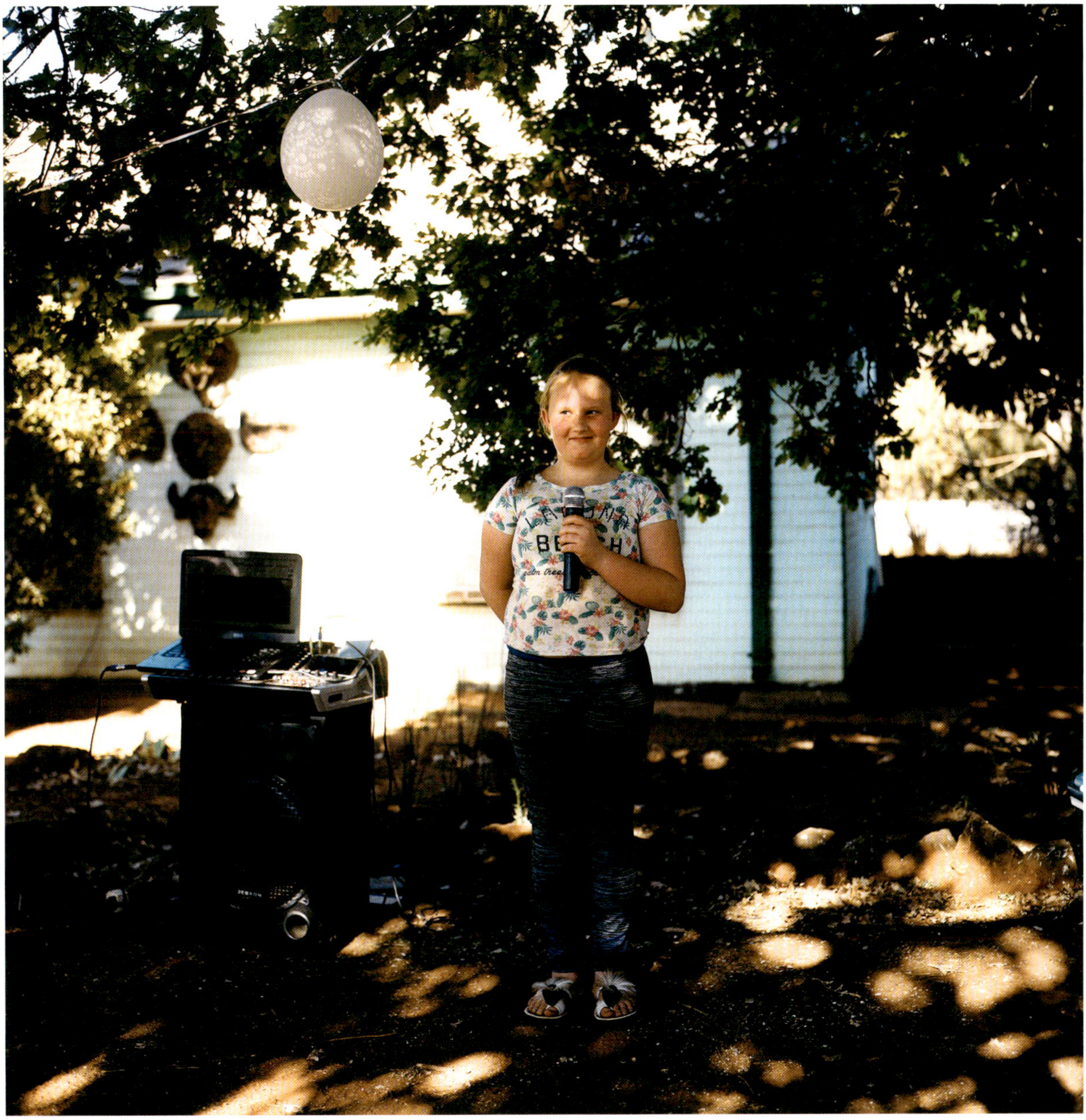

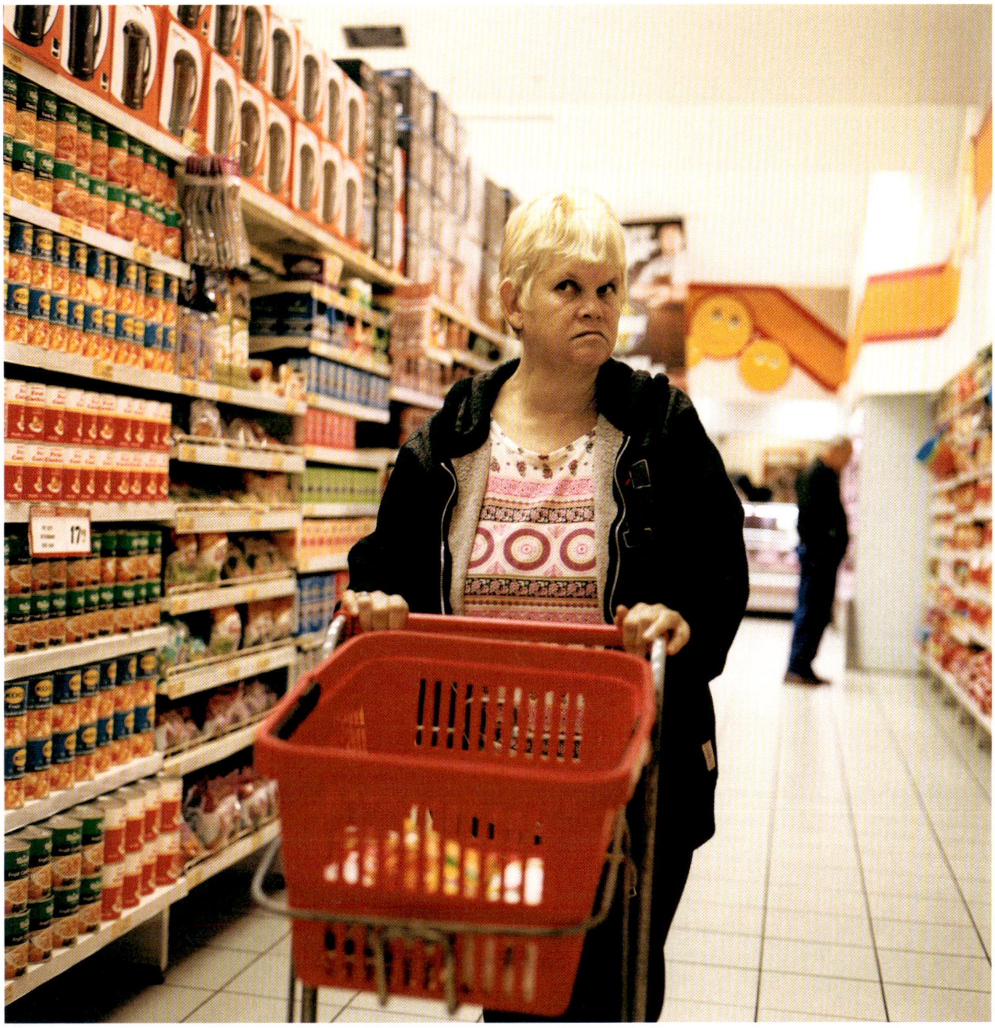

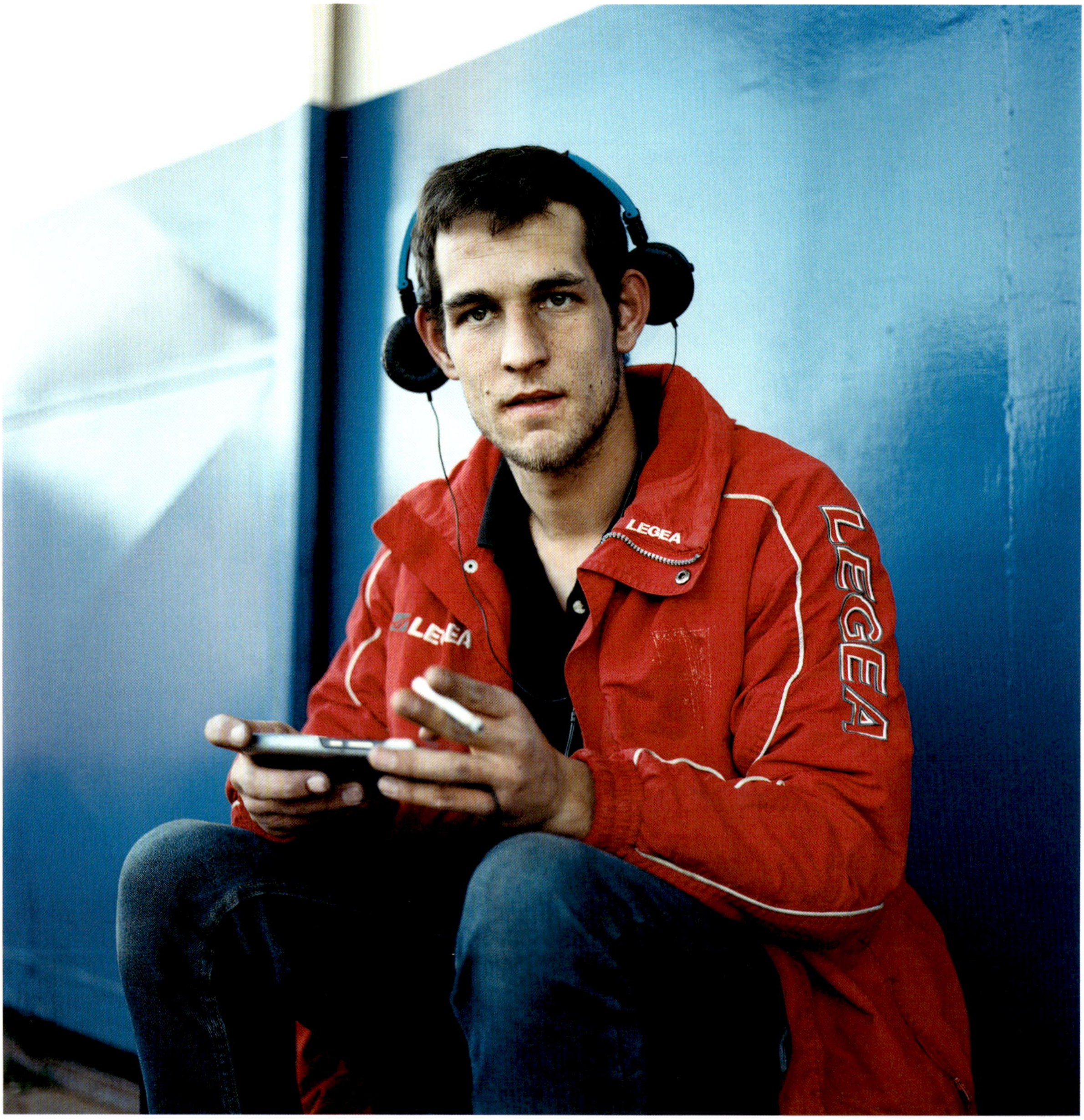
LEGEA
LEGEA
LEGEA

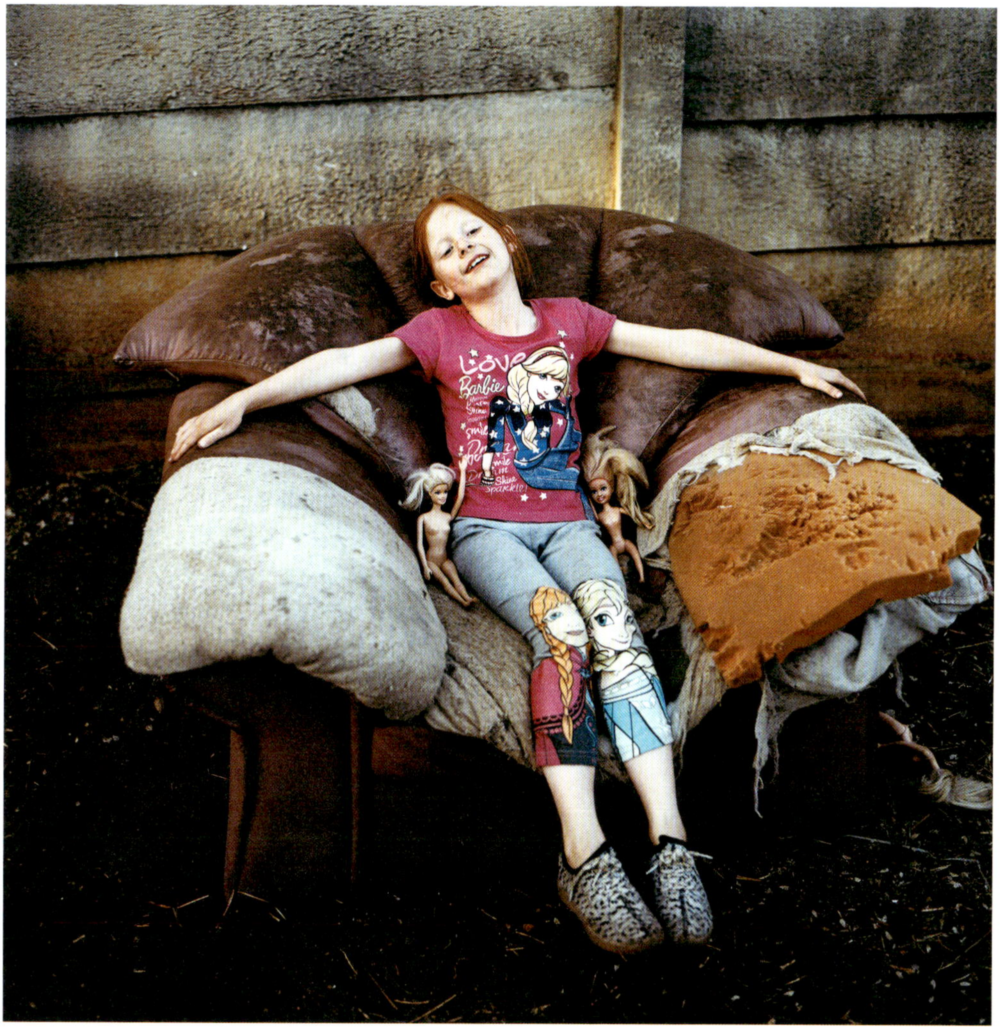
Love
Barbie

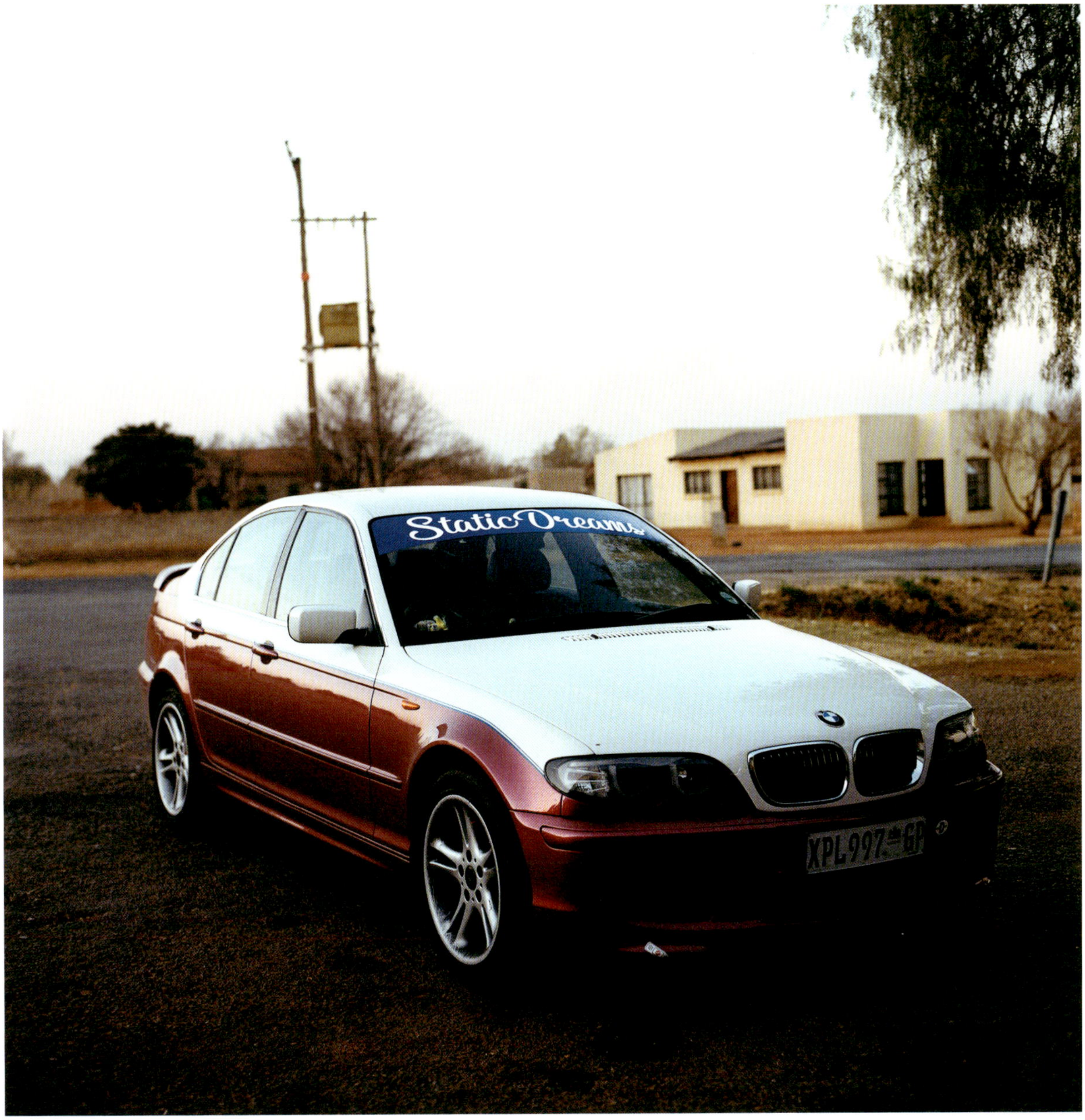
Static Dreams
XPL 997 GP

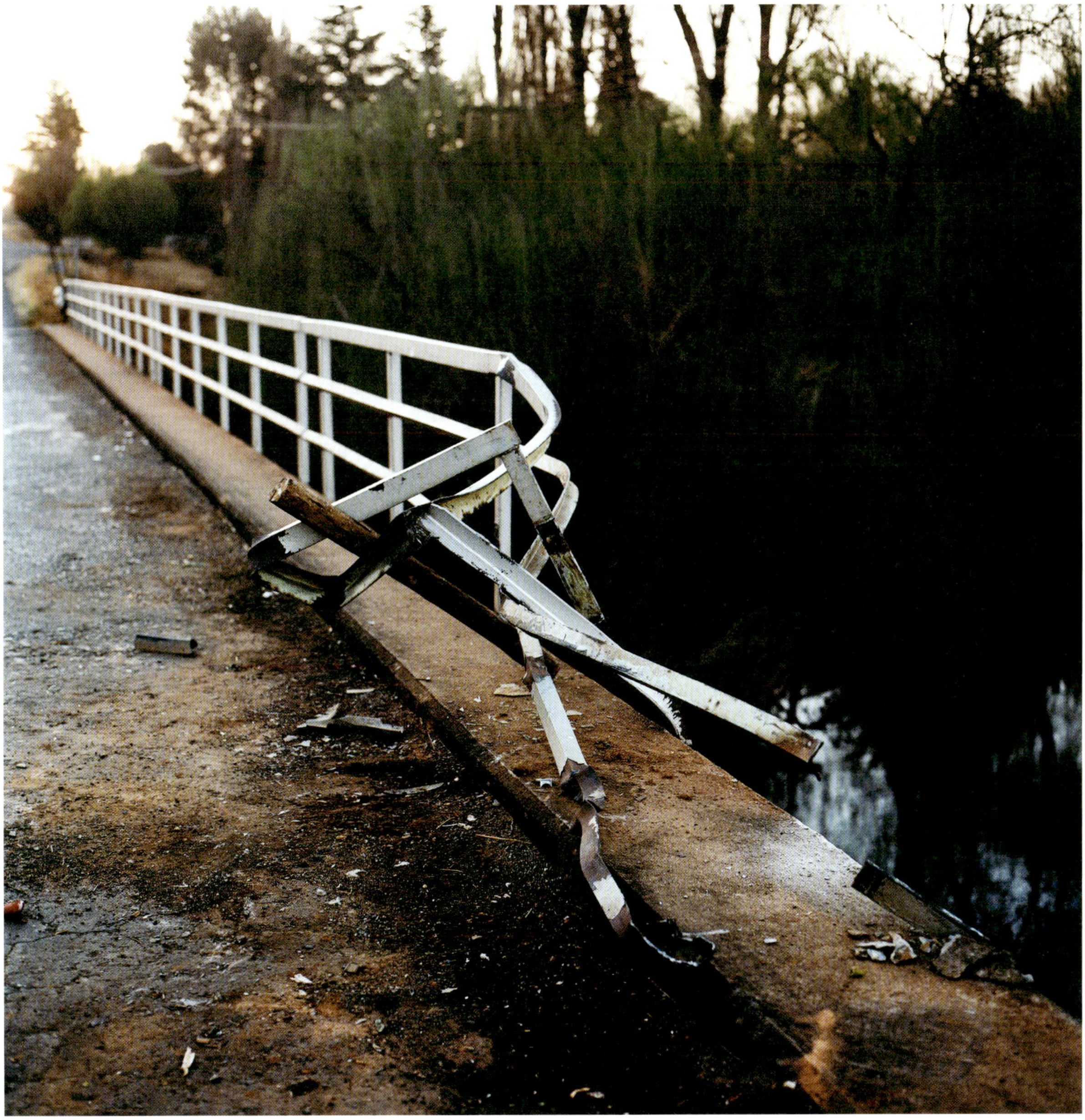

In 2015, intent of working together on a photographic project, Lindokuhle Sobekwa and Cyprien Clément-Delmas began visiting Daleside, a small settlement near the Klip River on the far-southern fringes of greater Johannesburg. Their manner of working was simple and exploratory. They initially hung out in Daleside's small commercial centre, in particular near the busy liquor store, observing the ebb and flow of civic life. They also explored the settlement's amorphous peri-urban landscapes, which bear the twin scars of commercial farming and opencast mining. Early on, they met a shirtless adolescent smoker named Brandon, who Sobekwa photographed in a fire-scarred landscape. They also met a burly pastor with a husky voice, who Clément-Delmas later portrayed ministering in a bold shirt design featuring a stud of horses. 'It's tough to survive in Daleside, but I love it here,' the friendly pastor told the photographers. A key ally in their project, he admitted that he had once been a member of a white supremacy group.

As time passed, the two photographers—Sobekwa, a Black man from nearby Thokoza, Clément-Delmas, a white man from faraway Paris—were accepted as familiar presences in Daleside. Their photographs, presented here side by side, in alliance as much as juxtaposition, unavoidably changed too. They became more intimate, less about the public instances of community in this ambiguously segregated settlement than the private rituals of family and youth. It was Sobekwa who had suggested to Clément-Delmas that they investigate Daleside. This little-known community, which since the post-apartheid remapping of South Africa's towns and villages has been absorbed into the sprawling Midvaal municipality, had long been an enigma for Sobekwa.

Nearly two decades ago, long before his 2012 discovery of photography in high school, Sobekwa's single-parent mother, Nomasindiso, took a job as a live-in domestic worker in Daleside. It was a stark choice for Nomasindiso, one that meant leaving her young boys in the care of their older sister, Ziyanda. On visits to his mother at work, Sobekwa offered to help with chores, but was told by the white homeowner not to enter her house. Much like his 2016 photo of two white adolescents, Jorden and Naiden, smoking in front of their peer, Bosman, who mows the lawn, Sobekwa spent his days outside. The racially motivated snub made Sobekwa curious. What secrets lay beyond the threshold of the stoep? What riches did the homes of Daleside's mostly white and seemingly affluent inhabitants hide?

Sobekwa and Clément-Delmas did not explicitly set out to examine racial privilege in post-apartheid South Africa, but their portrait-rich study of

DALESIDE: A SOCIAL HISTORY

Sean O'Toole

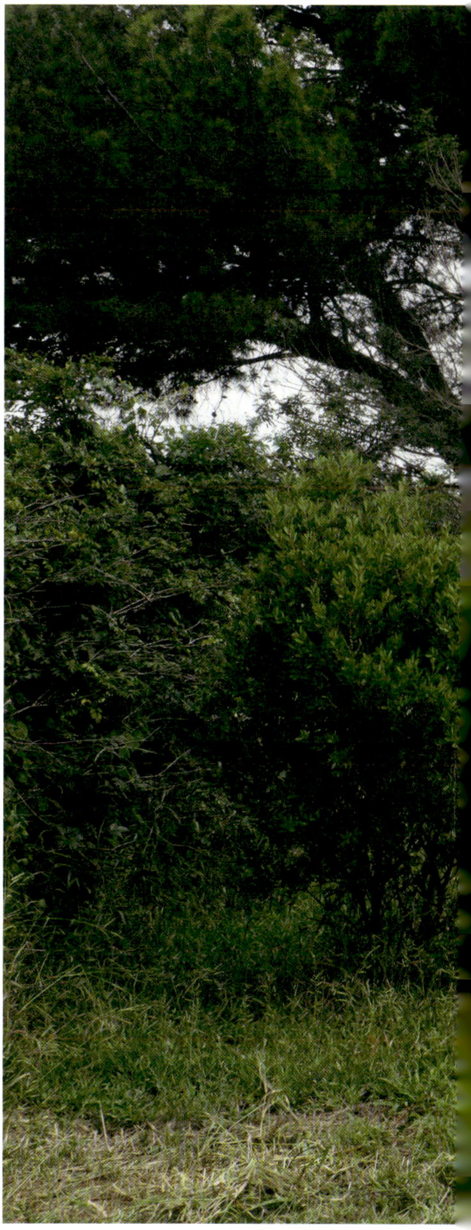

railway line with his family and beloved Miniature Pinschers. Even then the intimacies they partook in were tentative. Some white residents privately admitted their suspicions of Black South Africans to Clément-Delmas. Daleside is not unique in its prejudices. Old melancholies and ideological toxicities persist in the 'new' South Africa, which as a proposition remains a work in progress.

Youth, family and community, along with work, faith and leisure, are the dominant leitmotifs of Sobekwa and Clément-Delmas's photographic study of Daleside. Drawing on much-admired precedents of empathetic witnessing suggested by photographers like David Goldblatt, Santu Mofokeng and Alec Soth, the photographers have—persuasively and sympathetically—ended up visualising aspects of South Africa's unresolved interregnum. This Latinate word is not new to South African cultural and political discourse. The epigraph to Nadine Gordimer's 1981 novel *July's People* quoted Italian Marxist intellectual Antonio Gramsci: 'The old is dying and the new cannot be born; in this interregnum there arises a great diversity of morbid symptoms.' In a controversial 1983 essay Gordimer listed these morbid symptoms as including 'disintegrated consciousness,' 'contradictions' and 'internal friction.' Photography trades in surfaces, not immanent psychological states, but something of South Africa's inconclusive deferral is tangible in Sobekwa and Clément-Delmas's photographs.

The white subjects of Daleside commune and fret, while the few Black subjects portrayed, toil in subordinate roles. The endurance of old social regimes to do with work and land ownership is telling of South Africa's interregnum, but they are not the only markers of the protracted interval between a colonial past and postcolonial future. Youth is the prism through which the possibilities and challenges of life in present-day Daleside are most poignantly and reliably refracted. Clément-Delmas's portrait of two equal-aged boys posed outdoors—one is white, the other is Black and seated on an orange bicycle—registers youthful mutuality and cohabitation. It is an optimistic portrait of what in French is termed *vivre ensemble*. Identity, though, exceeds race. Dominique, the pubescent white girl who posed for Sobekwa on a pink crocheted blanket next to her abundantly decorated bedroom wall, dreams of being a glamour model. Other adolescent girls who sat for the photographers over the years are now young wives, mothers and staunch promoters of Jesus. Clément-Delmas's penultimate photo of a tricked-out BMW with a swirl of lettering affixed to the windscreen declaring 'Static Dreams' reads like an omen for all the youths of Daleside.

This book closes with an ambiguous pairing of photographs that attempt to process the hard-luck street philosophy proposed by the BMW while also, in formal terms, returning the reader to the subject of passage and labour introduced in the opening pairing of photographs. At right, Sobekwa's final frame offers a sidelong view of a greying woman mowing an overgrown lawn. The scene updates a well-known Goldblatt photo made during the twilight of apartheid in Boksburg, a former mining settlement located near Sobekwa's birthplace in Katlehong. There is housework to be done, Sobekwa's photo optimistically proposes, although Dominique may disagree. Presented opposite is a view of the bridge crossing the Klip River taken by Clément-Delmas. The bridge, a southern exit out of Daleside into the Free State province, shows signs of a violent accident. The bridge, though, is still operational.